A Guide to Jewish History Sources in the History Library of the Western Reserve Historical Society

THE CLEVELAND JEWISH ARCHIVES

A Guide to Jewish History Sources in the History Library of the Western Reserve Historical Society

Compiled by
John J. Grabowski
Lucinda K. Arnold

Edited by
Kermit J. Pike

The Western Reserve Historical Society
Cleveland, Ohio
1983

Cover illustration: The cover reproduces the Hebrew text of the opening page of the ethical testament given to the emigrants who left Unsleben, Bavaria, for Cleveland 21 Iyar 5599 (May 5, 1839); the text reads, "May God send His angel before you / May no ill befall you / In all your ways know Him / And He will make your paths straight." The manuscript is the oldest in the Cleveland Jewish Archives.

Copyright © by the Western Reserve Historical Society
All Rights Reserved
Printed in the United States of America
ISBN: 0-911704-30-2
The Western Reserve Historical Society Publication Number 160
Editorial design and supervision
by Kermit J. Pike and Roderick Boyd Porter
First Edition

Foreword

The Cleveland Jewish Archives was formally established in April 1976, with two equal grants provided by foundations representing the families of Rabbi Moses J. Gries and Mr. Leonard Ratner. In 1979, these foundations provided funds to allow the continuation of the archives for an additional year and to publish this guide. In planning and funding the archives, the support and cooperation of the Jewish Community Federation has been substantial.

The Historical Society is deeply indebted to the Lucille and Robert H. Gries Charity Fund and the Ratner, Miller, Shafran Foundation for their generous financial support of the Jewish Archives. From the Jewish Community Federation, Sidney Vincent, Howard Berger, and Judah Rubinstein were instrumental in developing the concept of the archives. In addition, Mr. Rubinstein has been most helpful in working with the archives staff to assure the preservation of historically important materials.

Special thanks are also due Ellen Gries Cole, who serves as chairperson of the special advisory committee to the Cleveland Jewish Archives. The members of this committee, drawn from all facets of the community, have been of great assistance in furthering the work of the archives.

The purpose of the Cleveland Jewish Archives, which operates as a special program of the History Library under the direction of Kermit J. Pike, is to collect, preserve, and make available for research the papers of Jewish individuals and families and the records of Jewish organizations and institutions that have had an impact on the growth and development of the Greater Cleveland area. In addition, the archives assists in the development of exhibitions, publications, and other means through which the information collected by the archives is disseminated to the community. The purpose of this guide is twofold. First, it is intended that it make known to potential scholars the scope of the resources of Cleveland Jewish history that are available in the Society's History Library. The second purpose is to acknowledge the generosity and cooperation extended by the many individuals and organizations which have chosen to serve the cause of history by donating papers and records to the Society.

In December 1981, the Jewish Community Federation established a permanent endowment fund through the initiative of David N. Myers, trustee of the Historical Society and past president of the Federation. Donors to the fund are The David and Inez Myers Fund, The Treu-Mart Fund, The Ratner, Miller, Shafran Foundation, The Lucille and Robert H. Gries Charitable Fund, and The Endowment Fund of the Jewish Community

Federation. The income from this archives fund will be made available to the Historical Society for the Cleveland Jewish Archives beginning in July 1984. Until that time, a special two and one-half year grant from the Cleveland Foundation and its Edith Anisfield-Wolf Fund will underwrite the cost of the archives.

On behalf of the Western Reserve Historical Society we are pleased to present this volume and look forward to the continuing growth of the Cleveland Jewish Archives and to the increased scholarly and public uses of the library.

THE WESTERN RESERVE HISTORICAL SOCIETY

Paul W. Walter
President
Board of Trustees

Theodore Anton Sande
Executive Director

Preface

This guide is a selective list and description of the major sources relating to the history of the Jewish community in Cleveland located in the History Library of the Western Reserve Historical Society. In addition to collections of papers of individuals and records of organizations and institutions, certain photographic and printed materials of potential research value have also been included.

The majority of the collections described here were acquired under the auspices of the Cleveland Jewish Archives. However, the guide also includes collections acquired before the establishment of the archives, as well as several collections received under other auspices but which contain material pertinent to the study of Cleveland Jewish history.

In preparing the descriptions for these collections, every effort has been made to reflect accurately the contents of each collection. Each entry consists of the name of the collection, followed by the nature of the material and the dates spanned, and the volume (by containers and linear feet). The name of the donor or source of the collection is followed by the call number assigned to the collection by the library.

The body of the entry begins with a biographical note on the individual or family in the case of personal papers or a brief historical note in the case of organizations and institutions. The description of the contents of the collection includes references to types of material found within each collection and lists of persons, places, events, and subjects to which references are made.

Lastly, the existence of a register (if available), microfilm edition, or restrictions is noted. In the several instances where access to the collection is controlled, the restrictions are given.

The publication of this volume represents the combined efforts of a number of people. Sandra Berman, the initial Cleveland Jewish Archivist, served the project with distinction during its phase of heavy acquisition. Mrs. Berman was succeeded by Ann Patterson and Lucinda K. Arnold. The latter prepared the first drafts of most of the entries in the guide. Fenn Fellows and students from the archives program at Case Western Reserve University processed many of the collections and prepared finding aids under the direction of Dennis Harrison, curator of manuscripts. The key person in the operation of the archives during the years has been John J. Grabowski, associate curator of manuscripts, who has been active in developing leads, negotiating the transfer of collections, and overseeing the project's special exhibitions and programs.

In every phase of the Cleveland Jewish Archives activities, including the preparation of this guide, Judah Rubinstein has been constantly helpful. In addition to discovering collections and acting as liaison with the Jewish Community Federation, he has been mentor and friend to all connected with the archives.

                              THE WESTERN RESERVE HISTORICAL SOCIETY
                              Kermit J. Pike
                              Director of the History Library

Note to Researchers

The Cleveland Jewish Archives is one of several special archival programs within the History Library of the Western Reserve Historical Society. The staff associated with each of these projects is responsible for the development of collections within a specific subject area, including urban, black, ethnic, and labor history. These serve to enhance the general collections of the library, which now include more than two hundred and twenty thousand volumes, one hundred and forty thousand photographs and prints, and two thousand manuscript collections. Although the bulk of these holdings relates primarily to the history of Cleveland and northeast Ohio, certain collections are national in scope. These include the anti-slavery movement, the Civil War, discovery and exploration, political campaigns, and American genealogy. Manuscript collections received by the library before 1971 are described in *Guide to the Manuscripts and Archives of the Western Reserve Historical Society* (1972), compiled by Kermit J. Pike and published by the Society. Researchers working within any topical area, including Jewish history, should consult this guide for descriptions of collections which may contain material relevant to their interest.

The History Library also holds a large volume of material useful for Jewish genealogical research. This includes microfilm of all the United States federal population census schedules from 1790 to 1900, as well as the Soundex (index) for the 1880 census, and the 1900 Soundex for Indiana, New York, Ohio, Pennsylvania, Virginia, and West Virginia. An index to birth, marriage, and death notices contained in the *Jewish Review and Observer* (1889-1954) is currently in preparation. Also available in the library is a listing of burials in the Willett Street Cemetery, the city's first Jewish cemetery. The library's growing oral history collection includes a series of two hundred and seventy-one cassette tapes of interviews conducted by the late David Miller, and a series of forty-five transcribed interviews relating to Jewish immigrant experiences conducted by the staff of the Jewish Community Center.

An important collection received when this guide was in the final stages of preparation is *Witness to Life (Ayduth Lachayim)*, biographical statements of Holocaust survivors residing in the Greater Cleveland area. A copy of this volume, prepared by the Jewish Community Federation, was presented to the archives at Yad Vashem during the World Gathering of Jewish Holocaust Survivors in Israel in 1981.

Contents

Foreword	vii
Preface	ix
Note to Researchers	xi
I. Manuscripts: Major Collections	1
II. Manuscripts: Vertical File Collections	41
Appendix A: Photographs	
1. Picture Groups	47
2. Portraits	53
3. Views & Events	57
Appendix B: Printed Materials	
1. Organizational	61
2. Published and Unpublished Studies	67
3. Newspapers and Periodicals	73
Index	75

I. Manuscripts: Major Collections

Each collection heading includes a title, general span dates for the material, number of containers and shelf space occupied in linear feet, provenance data, and the library's internal manuscript reference number for the collection. The entry format varies for items 69 through 79, which have been accessioned but not fully processed and catalogued.

The description of the collection provides historical or biographical information and comments on the nature of the materials.

Availability of finding aids and microfilm editions and the existence of restrictions to access are noted after the description.

Manuscripts:
Major Collections

1 HIRAM HOUSE. Records, 1893-1968. 76 containers, 2 oversize containers, 7 oversize volumes (38 linear feet). Donated by Mrs. George Bellamy and the Hiram House Camp, 1968-1972. MS 3319.

Hiram House, a Cleveland social settlement founded in 1896, played an important role in assisting immigrants, including Jews, to adjust to American society. From 1899 to 1941, Hiram House was located at East 27th Street and Orange Avenue. During the first two decades of this century the area was the center of the city's Jewish community. The establishment of the agency concerned some Jewish parents, who feared that Protestant settlement house workers might attempt to proselytize their children. Nevertheless, many Jewish immigrant children participated in Hiram House programs and activities.

The records include minutes of meetings, financial statements, ledger books, legal papers, employment and administrative policy documents, speeches, statements, proposals, publications, printed programs and flyers, scrapbooks, and photographs. The materials in this collection relate to a variety of local and national topics. Cleveland philanthropy is well-documented as are various social welfare themes associated with the progressive era. The records relate heavily to immigration and Americanization in Cleveland and reflect the experiences of several major ethnic groups in the city, especially Jews, Italians, and blacks.

Finding Aid: Unpublished 43-page register.

2 MAX SANDIN (1889-1971). Papers, 1918-1967. 1 container (0.5 linear feet). Donated by Irene Tennenbaum, 1972. MS 3542.

Seeking to escape induction into the Russian army, Max Sandin, who was born in Russia, immigrated to the United States in 1910 and arrived in Cleveland in November of that year. He worked as a peddler for a brief time and then obtained employment as a painter and paper hanger, becoming a member of a local union. Sandin was a conscientious objector during both world wars. Drafted during World War I, his non-compliance with orders resulted in a death sentence, which was later commuted by President Woodrow Wilson to a term in prison. Eventually pardoned from that sentence, Max Sandin continued his involvement in anti-war activities. He was associated with the American Civil Liberties Union, the War Resisters League, and the Fellowship of Reconciliation.

The papers include Max Sandin's autobiography, "I was Sentenced to be Shot"; correspondence and legal documents, 1918-1964; miscellaneous prose pieces written in both English and Yiddish; clippings and reprints of published articles; annotated calendars, 1955, 1961-1966; and miscellaneous publications. The materials in this collection concern Sandin's childhood in a Russian shtetl, immigration to the United States, anti-war activities, and prison experiences.

3 CLEVELAND SECTION, NATIONAL COUNCIL OF JEWISH WOMEN. Records, 1894-1967. 27 containers, 22 oversize volumes (13.3 linear feet). Donated by the Cleveland Section, National Council of Jewish Women, 1974. MS 3620.

The Cleveland Section, National Council of Jewish Women was organized in 1894 by members of the Ladies Benevolent Society, a sewing and social service group. The section was one of several belonging to the National Council of Jewish Women, which had been formed the year before in Chicago. The Council's major emphasis was philanthropic work both inside and outside the Jewish community. Following a fund-raising affair in 1897, the Council started the Council Educational Alliance, a settlement house whose major purpose was to Americanize Jewish immigrants. The Council Educational Alliance was one of the agencies that merged to form the Jewish Community Center in 1948. Over the years, the Cleveland Section has continued its work through integrated programs of education, service, and social action, sponsoring projects designed to meet the needs of the community.

The records include the by-laws and constitution of the National Council of Jewish Women; correspondence; minutes of the Board of Trustees and the Executive Committee, 1897-1964; annual reports, 1954-1965; newsletters, 1924-1964; financial records, 1929-1965; minutes of various committees and scrapbooks, 1894-1967; newspaper clippings, 1910-1965; and files relating to community service projects, such as Council Gardens (residence for older persons) and Hill House (mental health facility).

Finding Aid: Unpublished 16-page register.
Restrictions: Containers 6, 7, and 8 and volumes 20, 21, and 22 are open only with the permission of the Cleveland Section.

4 LEAGUE FOR HUMAN RIGHTS. Records, 1934-1945, 1949. 6 containers (2.5 linear feet). Donated by the Jewish Community Federation, 1974. MS 3632.

Organized in Cleveland in 1933 unde the leadership of Rabbi Abba Hillel Silver, the League for Human Rights' initial purposes were in line with those of similar undertakings in other American cities — to promote a boycott of goods produced under

Manuscripts: Major Collections

the newly created Nazi regime in Germany and to disseminate accurate information about anti-Semitic and dictatorial activities of that regime. During the mid-1930s, the League expanded its activities to emphasize combatting pro-Nazi and anti-Semitic activities in Cleveland and investigating local racial and ethnic discrimination. With the end of World War II, the League's general anti-discriminatory activities were carried on by other agencies; therefore, in 1946, the League dissolved. As one of its last activities the League published a pamphlet series, *This Is Cleveland,* which drew attention to the city's ethnic diversity.

The records include correspondence, publications, clippings, and files on the League's activities. The publications and other materials in the collection cover a broad span of topics, including the German-American Bund, the Silvershirts, the national anti-Nazi boycott movement, World War II preparedness, refugee relief, and immigration.

Finding Aid: Unpublished 10-page register.

Restrictions: This collection is available to the serious scholar publishing a book or an article for a scholarly journal or writing a dissertation. No duplication is permitted of the materials in this collection. An interview with the Curator of Manuscripts or the Director of the History Library is necessary to secure permission to use this collection.

5 HEBREW FREE LOAN ASSOCIATION. Records, 1904-1959. 5 containers, 5 oversize volumes (5.0 linear feet). Donated by the Hebrew Free Loan Association, 1975. MS 3640.

The Hebrew Free Loan Association was organized in 1903 when two prominent Cleveland businessmen, Charles Ettinger and Maurice Black, each contributed two hundred dollars to establish a fund to aid needy Jewish immigrants from Russia and Poland. The fund grew and on September 6, 1904, the Gmilus Chassodim Society or Hebrew Free Loan Association was established. Over the years, the agency's loan policies have varied. Although founded as an immigrant aid society, the Association transformed itself into a general relief agency by assisting the needy throughout the depression years. Since World War II, this agency has helped many individuals to finance education, start businesses, pursue new careers, and buy houses.

The records include the articles of incorporation, 1904; minute books of regular, quarterly, annual, and special meetings, 1906-1959; general account books, 1909-1925; loan listing books, 1905-1943; loan record books, 1908-1934 and 1943-1959; membership record books, 1907-1910, 1922-1929, and 1936-1939; correspondence, 1945-1959; reports and resolutions, 1932-1959;

memorials of deceased members, 1930-1945; and newspaper clippings, 1945-1959. The materials in this collection, especially the loan listing and loan record books, provide information about the economic and geographic mobility of immigrants in Cleveland.

Finding Aid: Unpublished 6-page register.

6 MORRIS ULLMAN FAMILY. Papers, 1857-1965. 2 containers (0.6 linear feet). Donated by Rufus M. Ullman, 1975. MS 3644.

Morris Ullman (1835-1908) was born in Buchau, Wurtemberg, Germany. In 1849, he immigrated to the United States, first settling in Philadelphia, then in Greensboro, North Carolina. After serving for a short time with the Confederate Army during the Civil War, Ullman was arrested in Chattanooga by the Union forces and charged with smuggling. He was confined in prison for more than a year. Upon his release, Ullman moved to Ohio, finally settling in Cleveland in the late 1860s. While previously residing in Youngstown, he, his brother Emmanuel, and cousin Leopold Einstein, began Ullman Brothers, a wholesale liquor business (later known as the Ullman, Einstein and Company). The business, which by 1919 was one of the largest liquor distilleries in the United States, was dissolved with the enactment of national prohibition. The family then turned to the sale of real estate and securities. Monroe A. Ullman (1866-1938), son of Morris Ullman, assisted by his son, Rufus, formed Ullman and Company, dealers in securities, and the Ullman and Einstein Realty Company.

The papers include personal and general correspondence, 1870-1919; financial papers, legal papers, and distillery formula books relating to the Ullman, Einstein and Company; and miscellaneous Ullman family receipts, certificates, newspaper clippings, and scrapbooks. Of special interest are the documents that concern Morris Ullman's trial and imprisonment for smuggling in 1863.

Finding Aid: Unpublished 4-page register.

7 UNITED TORCH SERVICES. Records, 1913-1974. 23 containers, 34 volumes (37.0 linear feet). Donated by the United Torch Services, 1974. MS 3646.

Formed in 1971, the United Torch Services of Greater Cleveland is the fundraising component of organized charitable and philanthropic work in Cleveland. It is the direct descendant of the Cleveland Community Chest (later the Community Fund and then the United Appeal) which was established in 1919. Be-

Manuscripts: Major Collections

fore World War I, both the raising and distribution of charitable monies was accomplished by the Federation for Charity and Philanthropy (later the Cleveland Welfare Federation and then the Federation for Community Planning), which was organized in 1913. The Federation for Charity and Philanthropy, in turn, had its roots in the Cleveland Chamber of Commerce's Committee on Benevolent Associations, which was organized in 1900. The United Torch Services and its predecessors often worked in close cooperation with the Federation of Jewish Charities that was formed in 1903 to raise and distribute funds for Jewish welfare work in Cleveland and elsewhere.

The records include minutes of meetings, printed brochures, and scrapbooks. These materials relate primarily to the founding and early development of the Community Fund, to the formation of the United Appeal in 1957, and to the agency's activities in the 1960s and 1970s. Documentation for other aspects of the organization's history is often sketchy. The scrapbooks, which pertain primarily to fund-raising activities during World War I, also touch upon Jewish charitable activity during the early years of this century.

Finding Aid: Unpublished 22-page register.
Restrictions: Limited access to financial records.

8 SIMON L. LIPSON FAMILY. Papers, 1885-1973. 1 container (0.5 linear feet). Donated by Leah Lipson, 1974 and 1975. MS 3649.

Immigrating to the United States from Russia in 1905, David Lipshitz, son of Rabbi Sander Lipshitz, arrived in Cleveland in 1906 and subsequently founded the Eagle Wholesale Grocery Company. In addition to being an ardent Zionist, David Lipshitz was one of the founders of the Hebrew school system in the city and active in the creation of the Cleveland Jewish Center complex in the Glenville neighborhood. Upon his death, the business was run by his sons Simon, Isaac, Jonah, and Lazar. The family name of Lipshitz was eventually Americanized to Lipson.

The papers include correspondence, miscellaneous prose and poetry, invitations, materials concerning the Eagle Wholesale Grocery Company, financial records and account books, printed items and newspaper clippings relating to the Lipson family. Much of the correspondence is that of Simon Lipson (1896-1974) who, like his father, was active in Jewish community life. He participated in the Cleveland Jewish Singing Society, the Zionist Organization of America, and the Jewish National Fund, and served on the board of the Cleveland Hebrew Schools. Simon's correspondents include friends, relatives, and editors of various

Cleveland newspapers. Some of the materials in this collection are in Hebrew and Yiddish.

9 SINAI SYNAGOGUE. Records, 1918-1954, 1961. 3 containers (1.7 linear feet). Donated by the Sinai Synagogue, 1976. MS 3652.

Sinai Synagogue was formally incorporated as Beth Hamedrosh Anshe Galicia (House of Learning, People of Galicia) on May 4, 1924. Originally established in 1899 as the Erster Galizianer Unterstützungs Verein (First Galician Aid Society), the organization provided both religious services and financial aid to immigrants from Galicia, Poland. By 1924, with immigration sharply curtailed, the society concentrated on religious activities. In 1956, the congregation of Beth Hamedrosh Anshe Galicia changed its name to Sinai Synagogue.

The records consist primarily of bound volumes, including minute books of regular, quarterly, annual, and special meetings, 1918-1953; minute books of the Galician Sisterhood, 1926-1941; a minute book of the Free Loan Society, 1938-1943; a notebook of the Society of Prayer, 1942-1953; a memorial record book, 1931-1952; financial and dues record books, 1918-1934; a cemetery record book, 1961; and membership lists, 1932-1942. Written for the most part in Yiddish, these records reflect various aspects of Jewish Orthodox life in Cleveland.

Finding Aid: Unpublished 3-page register.

10 SHOMREI HADATH CONGREGATION. Records, 1922-1974. 1 container, 1 oversize folder (0.3 linear feet). Donated by Arnold Oppenheim, 1974. MS 3653.

Founded as Shomrei Dath (Keepers of Faith) by Hungarian Jews in 1922, the name of this orthodox congregation was changed, according to its 1929 constitution, to Shomrei Hadath Congregation. At its peak the congregation had between five and six hundred members. Faced with a declining membership, Shomrei Hadath Congregation, the last Orthodox Jewish synagogue to be located within the limits of the city of Cleveland, merged with the Young Israel Congregation of Cleveland Heights in 1973.

The records include the constitution of the Shomrei Hadath Congregation, 1929; the by-laws of the Chevra Kadisha (burial society), 1929; minutes of regular and special meetings and financial reports, 1922-1932 and 1942-1974; lists of officers, miscellaneous records of the Chevra Kadisha, 1933 and 1945; various legal documents including deeds and mortgages, 1926-1947; letters relating to donations, 1945; publications of the congregation, 1924 and 1947; and newspaper clippings, 1953, 1972-1973.

*Manuscripts:
Major Collections*

Manuscripts:
Major Collections

11 SHIN MILLER. Manuscript, 1920-1922. 1 container (0.3 linear feet). Donated by Mrs. Shin Miller, 1974. MS 3654.

A copy of the draft of a 232-page unpublished manuscript, "House Divided," by Shin Miller, a Cleveland Jewish immigrant. The background of the novel is Jewish life in Cleveland during the early years of the twentieth century. Of special interest is the author's account of the Jewish movement eastward from the area of Woodland Avenue and East 22nd Street (Perry Street) and his comments regarding the impact on the Jewish community by the influx of blacks and Italians into the neighborhood.

12 SELMA H. WEISS (d. 1974). Papers, 1926-1946. 1 container (0.3 linear feet). Donated by Lillian W. Mohler, 1974. MS 3655.

Selma H. Weiss, a social worker, was active in both Jewish and non-Jewish social service agencies. Early in her career, she was assistant superintendent of the Hebrew Relief Association. Leaving that position, Weiss studied at the New York School of Social Work and then joined the staff of the Children's Aid Society of Philadelphia. In 1926, she returned to Cleveland to work for the Welfare Association for Jewish Children, a child placement agency. Acting as a hospital base director during World War II, she moved to Washington, D.C., to work for the American Red Cross.

The papers include correspondence, 1936; notes concerning a 1936 trip to the Soviet Union; miscellaneous materials regarding her social service activities, 1936 and 1945-1946; and newspaper clippings, 1926, 1936 and 1943. The notes and letters relating to Miss Weiss's journey to the Soviet Union contain lengthy references to the Soviet regime.

13 MARY B. GROSSMAN (1880-1977). Papers, 1921-1966. 2 containers (0.6 linear feet). Donated by Mrs. Edith Garver, 1976 and 1977. MS 3660.

Born in Cleveland of Hungarian immigrant parents, Mary B. Grossman was a graduate of Baldwin Wallace College in Berea and the Cleveland Law School. She was admitted to the Ohio bar in 1912 and was the first woman to practice in the Cleveland District Federal Court. She was also the first woman to join the Commercial Law League of America and one of the first women admitted to the American Bar Association. In addition, Grossman was elected Cleveland Municipal Judge in 1923, the first woman in the United States to serve in such a capacity. In 1932, she was admitted to practice before the United States Supreme Court.

Judge Grossman remained on the Cleveland municipal bench until 1960.

The papers include correspondence, 1932-1959; four scrapbooks devoted to Judge Grossman's election campaigns from 1923 to 1947; campaign materials, 1941 and 1947; certificates and awards, 1948-1968; and three scrapbooks of newspaper clippings, 1921-1934.

14 OAKWOOD CLUB. Records, 1872-1955. 1 container (0.5 linear feet). Donated by the Oakwood Club, 1976. MS 3661.

The Oakwood Club was established in 1905 as a Jewish country club. In 1931 the club absorbed the Excelsior Club, originally a Jewish men's social club organized in Cleveland in 1872. The resulting body maintained the name of the Oakwood Club and consolidated all activities at the Oakwood Club facilities at Warrensville Center and Mayfield roads. During World War II, the Oakwood Club turned over its clubhouse to the 729th Military Police Battalion from June 1943 until February 1944.

The records include the constitution and bylaws of the Excelsior Club, 1872; an account of the proceedings of the Board of Election of the Excelsior Club, 1893-1901; and minutes and presidents' reports of the Excelsior Club, 1899-1904. The collection also contains a history of the Oakwood-Excelsior merger and materials relating to the Oakwood Club, including constitutions of the Oakwood Club, 1930, 1935, 1941, 1946, and 1948; correspondence, 1914-1941; membership and subscription records of the Oakwood Club, 1905 and 1939-1944; and other miscellaneous items.

15 JEWISH VOCATIONAL SERVICE. Records, 1939-1966. 1 container, 1 oversize container (0.8 linear feet). Donated by the Jewish Vocational Service, 1976. MS 3663.

As a result of a joint recommendation of the Jewish Social Service Bureau and the Council Educational Alliance, the Jewish Vocational Service was established in 1939 to coordinate work done in vocational guidance and training and job placement. Both of these agencies, which had been functioning in this field for some time, recognized the need for a central autonomous agency. Since its establishment, the Jewish Vocational Service has given advice to thousands of individuals seeking employment, aided students in college and career selection, and has assisted many veterans and refugees to adjust to the Cleveland community and to find work.

The records consist primarily of minutes, 1939-1966, and correspondence, bulletins, brochures, and newspaper clippings.

Manuscripts: Major Collections

Also included are scrapbooks, 1939-1966.

Note: The minutes and related materials in this collection are machine-made copies of the originals.

16 BELLEFAIRE. Records, 1868-1972. 19 containers, 6 oversize volumes (7.9 linear feet). Donated by Bellefaire and the Jewish Orphan Home Alumni Association, 1976. MS 3665.

Organized in 1868 to care for Jewish orphan children in the Midwest, Bellefaire was originally incorporated in Cleveland as the Jewish Orphan Asylum. The home was the result of the efforts of the B'nai B'rith Grand Lodge District Two, which had earlier made the decision to tax all members in the district one dollar per year "in order to create a fund which some time in the near future might be used for the organization of a charitable or educational institute." By the 1920s, the emphasis of the Jewish Orphan Asylum began to shift from the care of orphan children to care for the emotionally troubled child. Its Woodland Avenue facility soon thereafter became inadequate to meet the changing needs of the home. By 1929, new facilities were constructed at Fairmount and Belvoir boulevards in University Heights. The name of the institution was changed to Bellefaire shortly after the move.

The records include minutes of the Board of Trustees and Directors and various other boards, committees, and agencies, 1876-1957; correspondence, 1880-1943; publications, including annual reports, 1869-1938, and the *Jewish Orphan Asylum Magazine* and its successors, 1903-1972; and scrapbooks 1879-1963. Of particular interest is a journal, 1910, written by Harry Goldman, resident of the home.

Finding Aid: Unpublished 15-page register.

17 JEWISH COMMUNITY CENTER OF CLEVELAND. Records, 1899-1965. 45 containers, 2 oversize containers (49.6 linear feet). Donated by the Jewish Community Center of Cleveland, 1975 and 1976. MS 3668.

The Jewish Community Center of Cleveland was established in 1948 after a group study sponsored by the Jewish Community Federation recommended the merger of four predecessor agencies: the Council Education Alliance, Camp Wise, the Jewish Young Adult Bureau, and the Cultural Department of the Jewish Community Council. Founded in 1899 by the Cleveland Section, National Council of Jewish Women, the Council Educational Alliance was organized as a settlement house in the Woodland

Avenue area, the heart of the immigrant community. When immigration decreased in the 1920s, the Alliance shifted its emphasis to activities such as athletics and social and cultural functions.

The Jewish Young Adult Bureau was formed in 1939 to meet the needs of many organized young adult groups that lacked facilities for meetings and activities. Throughout its existence, the Bureau coordinated cultural and recreational activities for more than fifty groups. When it merged in 1948 into the newly created Jewish Community Center, the bureau became the Young Adult Service Division.

Camp Wise was founded in 1907 to enable Jewish children of differing backgrounds to experience country living in a camp setting. After World War II, Camp Wise and another camp, Camp Henry Baker, were merged under the administration of the Council Educational Alliance.

The Cultural Department of the Jewish Community Council began in 1945 as an experiment in revitalizing Jewish cultural activities for adults. In October 1948, the department became part of the Adult Services Division of the Community Center.

From 1948 to 1959, the Jewish Community Center conducted all business and program activities at neighborhood branches, with its main branch on Kinsman Road near East 135th Street. In 1958, land was purchased at Taylor and Mayfield roads in Cleveland Heights; a new, modern facility was erected and all branch operations were closed.

The records include the files of the Council Educational Alliance, 1899-1953; the Jewish Young Adult Bureau, 1939-1949; Camp Wise, 1907-1964; Jewish Community Center central administration, 1948-1965; the branches, 1948-1960; the Jewish Community Center Division, 1948-1965; and publications.

The records of the Jewish Community Council are held by the Jewish Community Federation of Cleveland and are not part of this collection.

Finding Aid: Unpublished 67-page register.

Restrictions: Container 2 is open only with the permission of the Jewish Community Center.

18 ABRAHAM LINCOLN NEBEL, *collector.* Cleveland Jewish Miscellany, 1831-1971. 1 container (1.0 linear feet). Donated by Mr. and Mrs. Charles Cohen, 1976. MS 3669.

Born in Zanesville, Ohio, of Austro-Hungarian immigrant parents, Abraham Lincoln Nebel (1891-1973) moved to Cleveland with his family in 1900. Nebel quit school at the age of fifteen to

Manuscripts:
Major Collections

assist his family financially. With the help of his brother Emmanuel, he formed the Commonwealth Oil Company, the first chain of gas stations in the city. In 1915, this business was sold, and Abraham Nebel established the Nebel Manufacturing Company. In later years Nebel involved himself deeply in local history and research. His interest in his Jewish background and heritage inspired him to devote much of his spare time to collecting material relating to the history of the Jewish community in the Greater Cleveland area.

The collection includes correspondence, genealogical material, biographies, notes, newspaper clippings, and various documents relating to the individuals, businesses, and religious organizations in the Cleveland Jewish community. Nebel rarely collected original documents. The bulk of the collection consists of copies, with the exception of Nebel's personal notes and correspondence.

Finding Aid: Unpublished 7-page register.
Note: This collection is also available on microfilm (3 rolls).

19 SIEGFRIED EINSTEIN (b. 1846). Papers, 1856-1919. 1 container (0.2 linear feet). Donated by Mrs. Harold Ensten, 1976. MS 3671.

Having emigrated from Germany in 1864, Siegfried Einstein settled in Cleveland shortly after his arrival in the United States. He became a prominent entrepreneur in Cleveland business and was active in Jewish community affairs. Five years after his arrival, he received his citizenship papers.

The papers include the certificate of citizenship of Siegfried Einstein, 1869; correspondence, 1881-1931; Einstein's German emigration visa, 1864; newspaper clippings, 1906 and 1919; and other miscellaneous materials.

Note: Some of the items in this collection are in German.

20 BIKUR CHOLIM LADIES SICK AID SOCIETY. Records, 1900-1974. 2 containers, 1 oversize volume (0.7 linear feet). Donated by Mrs. Ben Palchick, 1976 and 1979. MS 3673.

The Bikur Cholim Ladies Sick Aid Society was organized in August 1900 for the purpose of providing monetary assistance to the indigent and visiting the sick. This volunteer organization, in addition to offering assistance to individuals in need, was the auxiliary of the Jewish Convalescent Home (later the Jewish Convalescent and Rehabilitation Center).

The records include the constitution and articles of incorporation, 1900; minutes of the Board of Trustees meetings,

1935-1950; correspondence, 1949-1969; financial documents, 1950-1969; certificates, 1945-1946 and 1950; programs, 1952-1974; newspaper clippings, 1943 and 1960; fund-raising campaign bulletins; and other miscellaneous printed items.

Note: Many of the earlier materials, including the minutes, are in Yiddish.

21 MAX P. GOODMAN FAMILY. Papers, 1867-1934. 1 container (0.3 linear feet). Donated by Mrs. Albert Levin, 1977. MS 3677.

Born in Cleveland of Austrian immigrant parents, Max P. Goodman (1872-1934) was an attorney, a Cleveland city councilman, a vice-president of the Ohio Bar Association and, from 1925 to 1928, the first president of the Cuyahoga County Bar Association. After several years of working as a musician and studying law in the offices of Charles and Peter Zucker, Goodman was admitted to the bar in 1895. He was particularly well known for his knowledge of laws governing building and loan associations and banks. Goodman was also active in Jewish affairs and, in 1903, served as president of the Young Men's Hebrew Association. In 1907, he was elected president of the Cleveland Chapter of the Order of B'nai B'rith. He was also a trustee of the Euclid Avenue Temple (Anshe Chesed Congregation) from 1921 to 1923 and was an active member of the Forest City Lodge, Free and Accepted Masons.

The papers include a 1934 memorial to Max P. Goodman, miscellaneous legal documents such as mortgages and deeds, financial records, certificates, naturalization papers, and a German emigration visa. The materials in this collection relate both to the life and career of Max Goodman and to the lives of his relatives, members of the Wagner and Bamberger families.

22 JOSEPH AND FEISS COMPANY. Records, 1847-1960. 5 containers, 1 oversize volume (6.4 linear feet). Donated by the Joseph and Feiss Company, 1977 and 1978. MS 3682 [3886].

Joseph and Feiss Company, a small general store, opened in Meadville, Pennsylvania, in 1841. It was operated by Caufman Koch and Samuel Loeb, who moved the store to Cleveland in 1845. As it prospered, the company, which specialized in tailored men's clothing, opened additional stores throughout the city.

By the mid-1860s, the firm's expansion and success required Koch to offer partnerships to other individuals, including Adolph Mayer, Jacob Levi, Jacob Goldsmith, Julius Feiss, and Moritz Joseph. The actual name of the business reflected the change in

Manuscripts: Major Collections

Manuscripts:
Major Collections

partnerships. The name successively changed from Koch, Levi, Mayer and Company in 1865; to Koch, Goldsmith and Company in 1872; to Koch, Goldsmith, Joseph and Company in 1873; to Goldsmith, Joseph, Feiss and Company in 1889; and finally to the Joseph and Feiss Company in 1907. Formally incorporated as the Joseph and Feiss Company in 1920, the business, through the efforts of one of its executives, Paul Feiss, was an active promoter of liberal employment policies for its workers. The company is now part of the Van Heusen Corporation.

The records include minutes of board of directors' meetings and of shareholders' meetings, 1920-1960; minutes of the foremen's council, 1919-1924; correspondence kept by Paul and Richard Feiss, 1877-1940; copies of newspaper articles, 1847-1948; reports, legal and financial materials, topical files, publications relating to the operation of the Joseph and Feiss Company for more than one hundred years; and one oversize payroll journal.

Finding Aid: Unpublished 9-page register.

23 SAMUEL H. SILBERT (1883-1976). Papers, 1902-1969. 17 containers (20.1 linear feet). Donated by Samuel Silbert, 1969. MS 3683.

Samuel H. Silbert was born in Riga, Latvia, and immigrated at the age of five with his family to Newark, New Jersey. After several moves, Silbert arrived in Cleveland in 1902. He obtained a law degree from Cleveland Law School in 1907 and engaged in private practice until 1912. He was then appointed police prosecutor by Newton D. Baker, mayor of Cleveland. He served in that position until 1915, when he was elected a judge of the municipal court. In 1924 Samuel Silbert was elected judge of the court of common pleas, a position he held until 1954 when the other judges of the bench selected him as chief justice. Judge Silbert retired from the bench in 1968 with the title of chief justice emeritus.

The papers include correspondence, 1905-1968; memoranda, 1941-1968; articles, 1924-1967; and speeches and autobiographical accounts. Also included are miscellaneous documents and business files. The materials in this collection reflect Silbert's life from his early experiences as a salesman through his many years as a jurist. Much of the correspondence, writings, and memoranda relate to judicial issues and cases. Some of the correspondence and memoranda concern Silbert's family. Many of these items were written specifically for Silbert's autobiography, *Judge Sam*, which was published in 1963.

Finding Aid: Unpublished 15-page register.

24 SHERITH ISRAEL OF MOUNT PLEASANT. Records, 1923-1954. 1 container (1.0 linear feet). Donated by the Warrensville Center Synagogue, 1978. MS 3689.

The Sherith Israel Congregation of Mount Pleasant was organized on May 31, 1922, to provide a place of worship for Orthodox Jews in the Mount Pleasant neighborhood of Cleveland. After 1930, however, the Sherith Israel Congregation declined when Jews began to move out of the Mount Pleasant area. By 1938, the congregation had only forty-two members. Despite its small size and limited resources, Sherith Israel remained independent until 1962. In that year, it merged with the larger Sherith Jacob Congregation, commonly known as the Eddy Road Jewish Center. In order to preserve the identity of both congregations, the merged group was called the Sherith Jacob Israel Congregation. This congregation in turn merged into the Warrensville Center Synagogue in 1970.

The records include minute books of the congregation, 1923-1947; income and expense ledgers, 1924-1931; and membership and dues record books, 1926-1954. There are also miscellaneous items including three letters and a deed. The records, written primarily in Yiddish, will be useful to the scholar interested in Jewish Orthodox life in Cleveland and the role of the synagogue in the Jewish community.

Finding Aid: Unpublished 2-page register.

Manuscripts: Major Collections

25 TETIEVER AHAVATH ACHIM ANSHE SFARD CONGREGATION. Records, 1940-1955. 1 container (0.2 linear feet). Donated by Thelma Berk, 1977. MS 3703.

In 1909, a small group of immigrants from Tetiyev, Russia, who were members of the Tetiever Social Benefit Society in Cleveland, formed their own congregation. In 1910, this Orthodox Jewish congregation purchased a house on East 40th Street where religious services were held until 1924. In 1959, Tetiever Ahavath Achim Anshe Sfard Congregation merged into the newly formed Warrensville Center Synagogue.

The records include one minute book, 1940-1945; two yahrzeit (memorial) record books, 1951; and miscellaneous items and printed materials.

26 KNESSETH ISRAEL CONGREGATION. Records, 1898-1955. 1 container (0.4 linear feet). Donated by Mitchell Kohn, 1978. MS 3704.

Knesseth Israel, an Orthodox Jewish congregation, was organized in Cleveland in 1887 by a small group of Eastern European immigrants. Despite a decline in membership in the 1920s, this congregation endeavored to retain its autonomous status. In 1956, Knesseth Israel Congregation became part of the Taylor Road Synagogue.

The records include a minute book of the Chevra Kadisha (burial society), 1898-1954; a minute book of the Knesseth Israel Congregation, 1944-1955; and miscellaneous materials which consist primarily of financial documents.

Note: The majority of the materials in this collection are in Yiddish.

27 SAMUEL RICKMAN (1850-1914). Papers, 1884-1916. 2 folders (0.1 linear feet). Donated by Howard Klein, 1976. MS 3707.

Samuel Rickman was born in Hungary and immigrated to Cleveland in 1872. Actively involved in the Cleveland Jewish community during the late 1890s, Rickman was a member of the Oheb Zedek congregation and a member of various lodges and charitable organizations. His wife, Hannah (1844-1911), also active in local Jewish affairs, was a member of the Hungarian Ladies' Aid Society and the Austro-Hungarian Ladies' Aid Society.

The papers include correspondence, account books, and receipts from the Independent Oddfellows and the Sons of Isaac Association.

28 EUGENE M. KLEIN FAMILY. Papers, 1851-1964. 1 container (0.2 linear feet). Donated by Mrs. Willard Weiss, 1976. MS 3709.

Born in Cleveland, Eugene M. Klein (1899-1968), a prominent businessman, studied at Western Reserve University and Cleveland Law School. After obtaining a law degree in 1921, he specialized in employer-employee relationships. Klein developed a unique pension plan in 1929 and organized Eugene M. Klein and Associates, pension consultants. Klein was also active in the Jewish community. He was the founding president (1959-1962) of the Brith Emeth Congregation, a trustee of Fairmount Temple (Anshe Chesed Congregation), a trustee of the Bureau of Jewish Education, first president of the United Jewish Religious Schools, co-chairman of the Jewish Welfare Fund Campaign, and national treasurer of the Joint Distribution Committee.

The papers include correspondence, 1906-1964; reports and studies, 1936; certificates and resolutions, 1861 and 1945; and newspaper clippings, 1959-1964. Also included are the letters and postcards of Cecile Schaffner, a relative, and a friendship book spanning the years 1851-1875, which contains signatures and writings from many early Cleveland Jewish settlers.

29 LINCOLN LITERARY SOCIETY. Records, 1907-1970. 1 container (0.4 linear feet). Donated by Louis Pearsol, 1976. MS 3712.

On January 15, 1906, a group of six high school students formed the Lincoln Literary Society to study, debate and discuss contemporary literary works. The club, which met at the Council Educational Alliance, had more than sixty members in its peak years. The Lincoln Literary Society still exists as a social club sponsoring activities in which the "alumni" take part.

The records include correspondence, 1925 and 1956-1970; anniversary books containing membership lists and minutes, 1952-1969; a membership book, 1953; rosters and membership lists, 1951-1973; a copy of the Society's newspaper, *The Lincoln*, 1912; newspaper clippings, 1916-1960; and writings and speeches, songs, poems, and miscellaneous materials relating to different programs and events sponsored by the Society.

30 JEWISH FAMILY SERVICE ASSOCIATION OF CLEVELAND, OHIO. Records, 1895-1974. 18 containers, 1 oversize folder (20.3 linear feet). Donated by the Jewish Family Service Association, 1976. MS 3716.

Originally established as the Hebrew Relief Association in 1875, this agency is one of the oldest continuing Jewish social service agencies in Cleveland. During the organization's early years volunteers helped immigrants to obtain employment and provided material relief to the needy. In the 1920s, the Association began providing professional casework services. In 1924, it was renamed the Jewish Social Service Bureau to indicate its new range of services. In 1943, the Bureau became the Jewish Family Service Association of Cleveland, Ohio.

The records include minutes, reports, correspondence, and financial records relating to the administration of the agency and its committees. There are also a large number of training files used in the education of social workers, speeches, research papers, and statistics, as well as the minutes, reports, and correspondence of agencies working with the Jewish Family Service Association. Also included are thirty-eight theses relating to a variety of social service topics written by student interns from the School of Applied Social Sciences at Western Reserve University.

Finding Aid: Unpublished 31-page register.

Restriction: This collection is open only with the permission of the Jewish Family Service Association of Cleveland.

31 JEWISH WAR VETERANS POST 14, CLEVELAND, OHIO. Records, 1936-1977. 3 containers, 1 oversize volume (2.1 linear feet). Donated by the Jewish War Veterans, Cleveland Post, 1977. MS 3726.

The Jewish War Veterans Post 14 was organized in Cleveland in April 1919. It was admitted to the Jewish War Veterans of the United States (established in 1896) in 1925 and has subsequently benefitted the Jewish community by its service activities and advocacy on behalf of Jewish causes.

The records include correspondence, 1938-1977; membership lists, 1940-1973; minutes of national and regional meetings, 1939-1976; constitutions, 1939 and 1962-1964; financial records, 1945-1971; news releases, 1940-1979; and speeches, certificates, clippings, scrapbooks, and publications. Of special interest are materials highlighting stands taken by the veterans on issues such as the emigration of Soviet Jews and Nazism.

Finding Aid: Unpublished 4-page register.

32 ZIONIST DISTRICT OF CLEVELAND OF THE ZIONIST ORGANIZATION OF AMERICA (ZOA). Records, 1962-1975. 1 container (1.3 linear feet). Donated by the Zionist District of Cleveland, 1977. MS 3734.

The Zionist District of Cleveland of the Zionist Organization of America (ZOA) was organized in 1966 by the merger of three previous districts, including the Temple on the Heights District and the Temple District. Since the establishment of the State of Israel in 1948, the national ZOA has refocused its activities, emphasizing fund raising, interpretation, and the dissemination of information on behalf of Israel. The Cleveland district's activities in these areas have included the honoring of political and public figures for their support of the Jewish state.

The records include brochures, correspondence, national and regional constitutions, minutes, paid invoices, pamphlets, resolutions, receipts, and newspaper clippings. Although this collection includes some records from the early 1960s, the bulk of the material covers the period 1966 to 1975. This collection gives insight into the relationship between the Cleveland Jewish community and the American Zionist organizations, and into the Jewish community's mobilization during the Arab-Israeli crises of 1967 and 1973.

Finding Aid: Unpublished 8-page register.

33 MENORAH PARK, JEWISH HOME FOR AGED. Records, 1906-1968. 16 containers, 85 oversize volumes, 1 oversize folder (24.7 linear feet). Donated by Menorah Park, Jewish Home for Aged, 1976. MS 3741.

Menorah Park, Jewish Home for Aged was established as the Jewish Orthodox Old Home in 1906. Commonly referred to as the Orthodox Old Home, the institution provides an Orthodox environment for its residents.

By 1940, it was one of the five largest Jewish old age homes in the country, drawing applicants from throughout Ohio and adjacent states. In 1950, the name was changed to the Jewish Orthodox Home for Aged. Menorah Park was added to the name in the 1960s when new facilities were erected on Cedar Road in Beachwood, Ohio. The R. H. Myers Apartments, specifically designed for the elderly, were added in 1978.

The records include a constitution, 1956; minutes, 1906-1965; correspondence, 1920-1950; applications for admittance, 1921-1946; financial records, 1908-1966; reports, 1931-1944; legal documents, 1923-1945; publications, 1934-1960; and naturalization certificates, newspaper clippings, and scrapbooks, 1921-1941. The records highlight the operation and growth of this early twentieth century Orthodox institution and chronicle the change in attitudes toward care of the aged through the decades.

Finding Aid: Unpublished 19-page register.

34 SUBURBAN TEMPLE. Records, 1948-1973. 7 containers, 3 oversize volumes (9.7 linear feet). Donated by the Suburban Temple, 1977. MS 3753.

The Suburban Temple, Beachwood, Ohio, was established on July 7, 1947, by a group dedicated to the moral and ethical values commonly associated with American Reform Judaism at the turn of the century. The articles of incorporation were filed on February 25, 1948. Suburban's founders, largely former members of The Temple (Tifereth Israel Congregation), initially limited the size of the new congregation. Gradually, limitations were relaxed and the membership grew.

The records include correspondence, 1948-1970; minutes of the board of trustees and annual meetings, 1948-1971; and financial documents, committee reports, newspaper clippings, membership lists, lesson plans, and publications. Of special significance are the board of trustees minutes which report the discussions and procedures that led to the founding of Suburban Temple and the construction of the temple's building, and a group of letters written to United States government officials concerning

Manuscripts: Major Collections

the Soviet Union's shipment of arms to Arab countries.
Finding Aid: Unpublished 13-page register.

35 MOSES J. GRIES FAMILY. Papers, 1860-1955. 1 container (0.4 linear feet). Donated by Robert D. Gries, 1976. MS 3756.

Moses J. Gries (1868-1918) served as rabbi of The Temple (Tifereth Israel Congregation) in Cleveland from 1892 to 1917. In 1898, he married Frances Hays, daughter of prominent Cleveland businessman and banker Kaufman Hays. Rabbi Gries was noted for his interest in social problems and religious reforms. During his rabbinate he developed closer ties between his congregation and the general community and moved Tifereth Israel to the liberal forefront of American Reform Judaism. During the early part of this century Rabbi Gries was considered by many to be the leading spokesman for the Jewish community of Cleveland.

The papers include correspondence of members of the Gries family, 1895-1911; an anonymous diary describing a trip to Europe in 1897; a memorandum and account book belonging to Kaufman Hays, 1916-1917; and a scrapbook of Robert H. Gries, son of Rabbi Gries. Also of note is a commemorative scrapbook which contains condolence cards, telegrams, and newspaper clippings on the occasion of the death of Frances Hays Gries Watters in 1933.

Note: Additional Gries Family papers are maintained in the American Jewish Archives at Hebrew Union College, Cincinnati, Ohio.

36 HENRY SPIRA (1863-1941). Papers, 1885-1941. 2 folders (0.1 linear feet). Donated by Mrs. Barry Friedman, 1978. MS 3760.

Born in Richwald, Hungary, Henry Spira immigrated in 1879 to central Ohio, where he worked as a peddler. He returned to Hungary in 1885 and went into the wholesale liquor business. In 1890, he again left Hungary, settled in Cleveland, and continued his work as a liquor merchant. In 1891, he established a foreign exchange and banking office, which included a steamship ticket agency. Located on lower Broadway, and then on Woodland Avenue, the Bank of Henry Spira, later known as the Spira Savings and Loan Association, served many immigrants.

The papers include scattered immigration and naturalization papers, passports, and other records relating to Spira's trips to and from Hungary and to Henry Spira's early years in this country. Also included is a folder of correspondence, certificates of stock, and miscellaneous papers pertaining to the Spira International Express Company, a foreign exchange firm, 1917-1929.

37 TAYLOR ROAD SYNAGOGUE. Records, 1919-1968. 9 containers (3.3 linear feet). Donated by the Taylor Road Synagogue, 1977. MS 3765.

The Taylor Road Synagogue is the largest Orthodox congregation in the Greater Cleveland area. It was formed in the early 1950s by the merger of several smaller, older congregations — Oheb Zedek, Chibas Jerusalem, Agudas B'nai Israel, Agudas Achim, Shaaray Torah, and Knesseth Israel — during the movement of the Jewish community from the city into the eastern suburbs.

The records consist of general and financial records, including account books, 1919-1947; ledgers, 1941-1957; monthly and quarterly financial statements, 1949-1952; deeds, 1942-1957; minutes, 1927-1953, and membership lists, invoices, and receipts of Shaaray Torah, Chibas Jerusalem, and Oheb Zedek.

38 GREEN ROAD SYNAGOGUE. Records, 1949-1976. 3 containers (2.1 linear feet). Donated by the Green Road Synagogue, 1977. MS 3786.

The Green Road Synagogue was originally established as the Anshei Marmaresher Congregation by Orthodox Jews from Marmaresh Sziget, Hungary, in 1910. The congregation eventually moved to Lancashire Road in Cleveland Heights where it was known as the Marmaresher Jewish Center. During the late 1960s the congregation entered into merger negotiations with the Heights Jewish Center. Differences concerning rabbinical authority and degrees of Orthodox practice could not be resolved, and the negotiations ended without result. The congregation moved to Green Road in 1972 and adopted its present name.

The records include minutes, 1949-1975; correspondence, 1951 and 1962-1975; and financial membership records which relate to the administration of the synagogue and the activities of its congregation. Files relating to the synagogue's annual picnic, its annual banquet, its religious school, and the merger negotiations with the Heights Jewish Center form substantial portions of the collection.

Finding Aid: Unpublished 5-page register.

39 FEDERATION FOR COMMUNITY PLANNING, CLEVELAND, OHIO. Records, 1913-1974. 52 containers, 13 volumes (64.0 linear feet). Donated by the Federation for Community Planning, 1975 to 1978. MS 3788.

Manuscripts: Major Collections

As a coordinating body for funding and directing private and public welfare work, the Federation for Community Planning's antecedents lie in the early years of the twentieth century. The Federation is the indirect descendant of the Cleveland Chamber of Commerce's Committee on Benevolent Associations, which was established in 1900 to regulate the solicitation of funds by the numerous philanthropic organizations in the city. The committee's work led to the creation of the Federation for Charity and Philanthropy in 1913. The formation of this organization was, in part, patterned after the Federation of Jewish Charities; in 1917, the Federation for Charity and Philanthropy merged with the Welfare Council of Cleveland to form the Welfare Federation of Cleveland, which became the Federation for Community Planning in 1972. In 1919, responsibility for fund solicitation, which had been previously vested in the Federation, was given over to the newly formed Cleveland Community Chest. Though its functions and activities have varied through the years, the Federation's present activities center largely on planning for the welfare needs of the community and fund allocation.

The records include minutes, correspondence, reports, clippings, and publications of the Federation for Community Planning, the Welfare Federation, the Federation for Charity and Philanthropy, and of the various bodies allied to those organizations. The major portion of this collection dates from 1940 to 1970 and relates primarily to the Welfare Federation of Cleveland. It includes information on Jewish agencies in Cleveland, such as the Jewish Family Service Association, the Jewish Community Center, and the Jewish Children's Bureau. The materials in this collection provide an excellent overall view of the systemization of welfare and philanthropy in Cleveland and provide a basis for understanding this movement on the national level as well.

Finding Aid: Unpublished 91-page register.

40 ALEXANDER MILLER (1902-1975). Papers, 1938-1975. 1 container (0.2 linear feet). Donated by David Miller, 1975-1977. MS 3789.

Dr. Alexander Miller was the chief of orthopedic surgery at Mt. Sinai Hospital and Suburban Community Hospital and was active in the Jewish community in Cleveland. In 1938, he trained as a flight surgeon and served in the United States Army Medical Corps from 1941 to 1946. In 1960, Dr. Miller and his wife, Ellen, began to raise funds for the hospital ship *Hope*. He also sailed on the ship and visited many countries, including Ecuador and Vietnam, where he practiced medicine and assisted in training physicians.

The papers include correspondence, 1958-1975, military service records, certificates, flyers, brochures, newspaper clippings, and a scrapbook concerning the *Hope*.

41 EDWARD BUDWIG FAMILY. Papers, 1857-1904. 2 folders (0.1 linear feet). Donated by Mrs. Allyn Kendis, 1978. MS 3791.

Edward Budwig, a Cleveland businessman, married Esther Thorman (1842-1907), the daughter of Simson Thorman, one of the first Jewish settlers in Cleveland, in 1862. Soon afterward he became a partner in S. Thorman and Company, which dealt in hides and furs. Budwig's business affairs were troubled. Suffering from ill health, he relocated in Mexico and then California without his wife. The prolonged separation ultimately led to their divorce and to his separation from S. Thorman and Company.

The papers include correspondence, 1866-1888, an agreement, a certificate, and account books. The correspondence was written primarily by Edward Budwig to his wife and children, and approximately one half of it is in German. The majority of the remaining materials relate to Budwig's relatives and friends.

42 ALFRED A. BENESCH (1879-1973). Papers, 1900-1973. 2 folders (0.1 linear feet). Donated by Mrs. George Rose, 1973 and 1977. MS 3792.

Alfred A. Benesch was born in Cleveland to Bohemian immigrant parents. A graduate of Harvard University, Benesch began a law practice in 1903 with Benjamin Starr and became one of the city's most prominent lawyers and civic leaders. He was elected to Cleveland city council in 1912 and served as the city's public safety director, 1914-1915. He served on the Cleveland board of education from 1925 until 1962 and was its president in 1933 and 1934. Benesch was very active in the Jewish community, serving on the boards of the Hebrew Relief Association, the Jewish Orphan Asylum, and the Jewish Community Federation, among others. Benesch, a national and international officer of the fraternal order of B'nai B'rith, opposed a quota system for Jewish students at Harvard University in 1922.

The papers include correspondence and letters of condolence, 1900-1973; college grade transcripts and biographical data, speeches and addresses that Benesch delivered over the years, tributes, certificates, and newspaper clippings of articles written by and about him.

*Manuscripts:
Major Collections*

43 MORRIS SHANMAN (1875-1943). Papers, 1920-1943, 1950, 1963-1964, 1977. 1 folder (0.1 linear feet). Donated by Mr. and Mrs. Sanford Rose, 1978. MS 3793.

Morris Shanman was born in Russia and immigrated to Cleveland in 1881. In 1898, he and his wife, Esther, established the M. D. Shanman Company, a wholesale dry goods business in downtown Cleveland. When he retired, Mr. Shanman devoted himself to civic, cultural, and religious activities. He was instrumental in raising funds for the Cleveland Jewish Center (Anshe Emeth Congregation) in the city's Glenville neighborhood, serving as the congregation's first president in its new location. Shanman also served as president of the Cleveland Hebrew Schools.

The papers include one letter, 1950; deeds and certificates of ownership, 1920-1926; a funeral sermon, 1943; dedication programs, 1963-1964; certificates of confirmation, 1926 and 1932; and newspaper clippings.

44 EZRA SHAPIRO (1903-1977). Papers, 1892-1977. 2 folders (0.2 linear feet). Donated by Rena Blumberg, 1977. MS 3794.

Ezra Shapiro was born in Voloszhin, Poland, and was brought to Cleveland by his parents in 1906. A graduate of Ohio Northern University, Shapiro was appointed law director of Cleveland in 1933. He returned to private practice in 1935. Active in the field of Jewish education, he served as president of both the Cleveland Hebrew Schools and the Bureau of Jewish Education. He later became vice-president of the American Association for Jewish Education in 1959 and 1966. Shapiro became president of the Zionist District of Cleveland in 1924 and ten years later was elected to chair the national executive committee of the Zionist Organization of America. He was a founder of the American Jewish League for Israel in 1960, a non-politically affiliated Zionist organization in the United States. From 1942 to 1945 he was president of the Jewish Community Council. In 1971 Ezra Shapiro moved to Israel, where he became head of the Keren Hayesod-United Israel Appeal.

The papers include correspondence, 1892-1977; a brief biographical sketch of Ezra Shapiro, undated; speeches, 1970-1976; and tributes and eulogies delivered after Shapiro's death in 1977. The collection also contains certificates, newspaper clippings, and miscellaneous items.

Note: All materials in this collection are machine-made copies.

45 MAX APPLE (b. 1897). Papers, 1940-1971. 1 folder (0.1 linear feet). Donated by Max Apple, 1977 and 1978. MS 3795.

Max Apple, a businessman and community leader, has been active particularly in local Zionist affairs. After retiring from his paint and wallpaper business, he devoted much of his time and interest to Gan Yavne, a children's village he helped to found in Israel. Mr. Apple is a life trustee of the Jewish Community Federation and the Bureau of Jewish Education and has gained wide recognition for his philanthropic efforts.

The papers include correspondence, 1951-1971; certificates, 1953-1954; announcements and programs, 1941-1971; newspaper clippings, and miscellaneous printed materials.

46 WOMEN'S AMERICAN ORGANIZATION FOR REHABILITATION THROUGH TRAINING, CLEVELAND REGION. Records, 1965-1976. 2 containers, 2 oversize containers (1.1 linear feet). Donated by Mrs. Earle Lefton and Mrs. Allen Gart, 1976. MS 3796.

The Women's American Organization for Rehabilitation through Training (ORT) is a global organization that supports vocational training for Jewish immigrants and underprivileged in Israel and many other countries. The Women's American ORT was established in 1927, and the Cleveland Region ORT in 1957. Locally, ORT currently has five thousand members in twenty-eight chapters.

The records include correspondence, 1972-1975; materials concerning the history of the ORT; minutes of meetings of the Regional Board and the Executive Committee, 1972-1974; reports of the Cleveland Region made at various conferences and seminars, 1965-1975; newsletters, 1971-1976; and programs, fund raising manuals, certificates, newspaper clippings, and miscellaneous printed materials. Also included are two scrapbooks of newspaper clippings and printed circulars, 1972-1973.

47 SAMUEL NESHKIN (1898-1980). Scrapbooks, 1917-1977. 2 oversize containers (0.4 linear feet). Donated by Samuel Neshkin, 1978. MS 3804.

Born in Russia, Samuel Neshkin came to Cleveland in 1910. He became a tailor and eventually acquired and managed a clothing store. Neshkin is known primarily for his contributions to the Yiddish theater in Cleveland. Spanning six decades, this deep involvement included acting, producing, and directing.

The scrapbooks contain handbills, newspaper clippings, photographs, programs, and other memorabilia relating primarily to the Yiddish theater in Cleveland.

*Manuscripts:
Major Collections*

Manuscripts:
Major Collections

48 MANUEL LEVINE (1881-1939). Papers, 1908-1965. 2 containers (0.8 linear feet). Donated by Mrs. Mitzi Verne and Robert Levine, 1972, 1975, and 1977. MS 3805.

Manuel Levine emigrated from Russia to the United States at the age of sixteen. After studying law, he began his career in 1903 as assistant police prosecutor. In 1907, he was elected judge of the police court where he formed the first probation department in Ohio. Levine was judge of the Cleveland municipal court from 1911 to 1914 and a judge of the Cuyahoga County common pleas court from 1914 to 1923. In 1923, he was appointed to the court of appeals and, in 1931, became its chief justice. Levine also started one of the earliest citizenship classes in the United States at Hiram House social settlement in 1908 and served as the president of the Cleveland Immigration League.

The papers include correspondence, 1912-1932; speeches made by and about Levine; reports and legal documents; and financial records, such as bills of sale and receipts. The collection also contains scrapbooks of newspaper clippings, most of which relate to the career of Judge Levine and to developments in the legal profession in the 1920s and 1930s.

49 SIGMUND BRAVERMAN (1894-1960). Papers, 1936-1965. 3 containers (2.0 linear feet). Donated by Mrs. Sigmund Braverman, 1977. MS 3807.

Born in Austria-Hungary, Sigmund Braverman, an architect, demonstrated his Jewish heritage both in the buildings he designed and through his involvement in various activities in the Cleveland Jewish community. He came to the United States with his parents and settled in Pennsylvania. He attended the Carnegie Institute of Technology in Pittsburgh and obtained his degree from that institution in 1917. After serving in World War I, he moved to Cleveland in 1920 and opened his architectural offices. He was Cleveland's city architect from 1923 to 1935. During his forty years of practice, especially while associated with architect Moses Halperin, Braverman gained special recognition for the many synagogues he designed or assisted in designing.

The papers include correspondence, 1939-1959; drafts of speeches and articles on architecture and the notes used in their preparation, 1945-1960; newspaper clippings, 1936-1965; programs from dedication ceremonies and conferences; and prints and drawings of several of the structures designed by his firm. The materials in this collection relate primarily to Braverman's architectural projects, especially his work on synagogues in Cleveland and elsewhere throughout the country.

Finding Aid: Unpublished 6-page register.

50 JOSEPH WEINBERG (1891-1977). Papers, 1910-1976. 2 containers, 1 volume (3.3 linear feet). Donated by Mrs. Joseph Weinberg, 1977. MS 3812.

Joseph Weinberg was a prominent Cleveland architect. His family settled in Cleveland in 1901. When his father died, Weinberg was placed in the Jewish Orphan Home. After graduating from Harvard University with a degree in architectural design, Weinberg returned to Cleveland in 1913 and opened an architectural practice which, by the mid-1920s, specialized in large scale private and public housing projects. As senior partner of the firm of Weinberg, Teare and Herman, he collaborated on the design and building of many structures located in Cleveland and surrounding communities. Joseph Weinberg also served on the faculty of Western Reserve Univeristy and of the John Huntington Polytechnic Institute. His prominence as an architect was recognized many times, most notably when he received the American Institute of Architects Award of Merit in 1955 and the Architects Society of Ohio Gold Medal in 1974.

The papers include correspondence, 1910-1975; greeting cards, 1947-1974; school assignments completed by Weinberg and reports issued by organizations in which Weinberg was active, 1913-1967; certificates, 1921-1974; programs, 1924-1974; and bulletins. In addition, there are items relating to a number of reunions of Weinberg's 1912 graduating class from Harvard and materials on national and state architects' conventions which Weinberg attended. This collection also includes five scrapbooks, miscellaneous newspaper clippings about Joseph Weinberg's work or about subjects of particular interest to him, and designs, drawings, and sketches done by Weinberg during his years of training and professional practice.

Finding Aid: Unpublished 4-page register.

51 MARCUS ROSENWASSER (1846-1910). Papers, 1863-1911. 1 container (0.5 linear feet). Donated by Mrs. James A. Donovan, Jr., 1979. MS 3816.

Marcus Rosenwasser immigrated at an early age from Bohemia to the United States with his family. Encouraged by his family to go abroad to study medicine, Rosenwasser attended schools in Prague and Vienna before graduating from Wurtzburg in 1867. Returning to Cleveland in 1868, he opened a medical practice, specializing in women's diseases and abdominal surgery. He was a co-founder of Cleveland General Hospital (now St. Luke's Hospital), and gynecologist at Mt. Sinai Hospital and St. John's Hospital, physician in the Jewish Orphan Asylum, and president of the Cleveland Board of Health in 1901 and 1902.

The papers include tributes to Dr. Rosenwasser upon his death, 1910; brief biographical sketches of Rosenwasser and other members of his family; correspondence, 1863-1910; notes written by and about Rosenwasser; and a diary, 1864-1868, during which period Rosenwasser studied medicine in Europe.

52 SUGGS GARBER (b. 1895). Papers, 1920-1978. 1 container (0.5 linear feet). Donated by Suggs Garber, 1979. MS 3818.

Born in Latvia, Suggs Garber immigrated to the United States and arrived in Cleveland in 1905. Graduating from Cleveland Law School in 1921, he went into private practice and became the senior member of the firm of Garber, Simon, Haiman, Gutfield, Wertheimer, and Friedman. Mr. Garber was also very active in Jewish and Zionist-related activities as a member of such bodies as the executive committee of the Cleveland Chapter of the American Jewish Congress, the National Administrative Committee of the Zionist Organization of America, the board of trustees of Park Synagogue, and the board of governors of the American Association for Jewish Education. In addition, he served in varying capacities in the Cleveland Hebrew Schools, the Bureau of Jewish Education, the Jewish Community Federation, and the Jewish National Fund of Cleveland.

The papers include correspondence, 1943-1978; materials relating to American Zion Commonwealth, Inc. (a company founded to sell land in Palestine), 1920-1943; and items relating to tributes honoring Suggs Garber by the Jewish National Fund in 1962 and the Jewish Theological Seminary in 1976. Also included are certificates, newspaper clippings, and articles relating to Garber's work in the legal profession and his involvement in the Jewish community.

53 JEANETTE SHEIFER (1893-1979). Papers, 1921-1979. 1 container (0.5 linear feet). Donated by Mrs. Irving Hand, 1979. MS 3819.

Born in Rochester, New York, Jeanette Sheifer was a co-organizer of the Jewish Day Nursery of Cleveland and served as the first superintendent of that agency. She graduated from college in Montreal, Canada, and worked there before arriving in Cleveland. In 1921, with the aid of one assistant and a custodian, she opened the Jewish Day Nursery, accepting children from infancy up to age fourteen. In addition to running the nursery for the next twenty-five years, Sheifer was also involved in civic work and intergroup relations. She was a member of the Women's Zionist Organization and the Cleveland Association for Nursery Education.

The papers include correspondence, 1921-1979; minutes, agreements, certificates, reports, and membership cards illustrating Jeanette Sheifer's involvement in the nursery and the Jewish community; a brief history of the Jewish Day Nursery, undated; and miscellaneous invitations, bulletins, newsletters, and newspaper clippings.

54 MORRIS L. BERMAN (1898-1979). Papers, 1913-1947. 1 container (0.3 linear feet). Donated by Mrs. Morris Berman, 1979. MS 3820.

Born in Kiev, Russia, Morris L. Berman arrived in Cleveland in 1916 and went to work for the Kichler Company as a designer and decorator. He served in the United States Army in 1918-1919. In 1922, Berman started a pleating and stitching firm which became the Quality Thread Company, one of the largest distributors of industrial sewing thread in the country. He also started the Meistergram Company in 1933 and operated a hemstitching department in the May Company department store. A member of Fairmount Temple, he was active in the fund-raising campaigns of the Jewish Community Federation and helped to bring families to the United States from Europe.

The papers include correspondence, 1913-1947; and a diary kept by Morris Berman while serving in the Army in 1918. Most of the correspondence, portions of which are in Yiddish, dates from the years he served in the army.

55 L. N. GROSS COMPANY. Records, 1913-1962. 1 container, 4 oversize containers (4.0 linear feet). Donated by Louis N. Gross II, 1976. MS 3823.

Founded in 1898 by Louis N. Gross, who had emigrated from Russia, the L. N. Gross Company of Cleveland manufactures women's apparel. Among this company's several predecessors were Silber and Gross and, later, Gross and Dallet. The company has also operated several branches, including one located in Kent, Ohio.

The records include a history of the L. N. Gross Company, 1967; an autobiography of Louis Gross, undated; correspondence, 1914-1958; and reports, applications for patents, contracts made with other companies, and account books. Also included are four scrapbooks of advertisements and newspaper clippings, 1928-1962.

Manuscripts: Major Collections

56 CHARLES AUERBACH (1899-1979). Papers, 1935-1978. 3 containers (3.3 linear feet). Donated by David Auerbach, 1979. MS 3824.

Charles Auerbach, a Cleveland attorney, educator, and Zionist leader, was born in the Ukraine. Arriving in Cleveland in 1909, he earned a law degree from Western Reserve University and then studied at Harvard University. In 1922, he was admitted to the bar and practiced law for ten years with Max Goodman. Auerbach taught for thirty years at the John Marshall Law School, beginning in 1944. In addition to his work as a lawyer and professor of law, Auerbach campaigned in many communities for the United Jewish Appeal on behalf of Israel. He was a member of the executive committee of the Jewish Community Council and was a leading member of the Council's arbitration courts. Auerbach also was an author, writing works on the Talmud, Martin Buber, and on the American legal system.

The papers include correspondence, 1935-1976; writings on Jewish and legal topics and the notes and transcripts used in their preparation, 1940-1975; certificates, 1967-1974; newspaper clippings, 1943-1978; bulletins, publications, and articles and speeches by other individuals. These materials relate to Auerbach's legal work and his Jewish and Zionist interests. Also included are papers concerning the involvement of Auerbach's wife, Celia, in Hadassah and other Jewish women's organizations.

Finding Aid: Unpublished 5-page register.

57 LOUIS SKOLNIK (1890-1973). Papers, 1907-1974. 7 containers (6.8 linear feet). Donated by Leonard and Marvin Skolnik, 1974. MS 3825.

Louis Skolnik was a leader in the labor Zionist movement in Cleveland. He was born to Russian immigrant parents in London, England. At the age of one he returned to Russia with his parents, remaining there until 1905 when the family moved to the United States. The family initially settled in Newark, New Jersey, where Skolnik's father established a stair building company. Skolnik assisted in the work and learned the rudiments of carpentry. In 1914 Skolnik followed his older brother, Max, to Cleveland. Following his marriage in 1915, Skolnik established himself as a carpenter and contractor and eventually trained himself as an architect. Skolnik devoted himself ardently to Zionism, particularly labor Zionism. He was also active in various socialist and Yiddish cultural organizations. In 1966 Skolnik and his wife moved to Israel, where he died in 1973.

The papers, the majority of which are in Yiddish, consist

primarily of correspondence between Skolnik and the various Zionist organizations in which he was active. Included in the correspondence are letters from David Pinski as well as other leaders in the Zionist and Yiddish cultural movements. Certain records, including minutes, of Branch 45 of the Farband Labor Zionist Organization are also present in the collection.

Finding Aid: Unpublished 8-page register.

58 JULIUS AMBER (1907-1979). Papers, 1948-1979. 2 containers (1.5 linear feet). Donated by Mrs. Michael Phillips, 1979. MS 3827.

Born in Sokoly, Poland, Julius Amber came to the United States with his family in 1920. In addition to a long and distinguished career as a Cleveland attorney, Amber was active in the Jewish community. For several decades he was associated with the Jewish National Fund, of which he served as secretary from 1942 to 1953. In 1955 he was elected president of that body and held the office until his death. In 1967, Amber was elected honorary national chairman of the Jewish National Fund.

The papers include correspondence, 1963-1979; speeches, 1948-1979; and reports, biographical sketches of prominent individuals, invitations, programs, certificates, newspaper clippings, and published articles. Most of the materials in this collection relate to the Jewish National Fund on both the national and local level.

59 OHIO B'NAI B'RITH YOUTH ORGANIZATION. Records, 1947-1964. 5 containers (4.7 linear feet). Donated by Dr. Alan Riga, 1977. MS 3830.

The Ohio B'nai B'rith Youth Organization (BBYO) had its beginnings in Cleveland in 1932 when Emanuel Stern was asked by the National B'nai B'rith Youth Organization to form a service and social organization in Cleveland for Jewish youth. With the support of the Heights Lodge of the B'nai B'rith, Stern organized a group for boys which was called the Northeastern Ohio Council. This council, encompassing chapters in Cleveland, Canton, Elyria-Lorain, and Steubenville, later became known as the Greater Ohio Council (or Region); it was in turn joined with the Southern Ohio Council to form the Ohio B'nai B'rith Youth Organization. Centered in Cleveland, this organization subsequently formed many other chapters throughout the state.

The records include the office files of the BBYO director; administrative records, such as constitutions and correspondence; and program materials, including local and national publications and posters. The records in this collection provide information on the national organization in addition to the state and local chapters. Most of the materials, which date from the years 1958 to 1961, reflect the administration and evolution of a Jewish youth group from both a national and local perspective.

Finding Aid: Unpublished 11-page register.

60 BUREAU OF JEWISH EDUCATION. Records, 1924-1966. 16 containers, 1 oversize (21.8 linear feet). Donated by the Bureau of Jewish Education, 1977 and 1980. MS 3832.

The Bureau of Jewish Education is a constituent agency of the Jewish Community Federation and is affiliated with the American Association for Jewish Education. Organized in 1924, the Bureau's major function is to coordinate the activities of its affiliates, which include the Cleveland Hebrew Schools, the Hebrew Academy, the Cleveland College of Jewish Studies, the United Jewish Religious Schools, the Workmen's Circle School, the Yeshivath Adath B'nai Israel, Agnon Day School, and Akiva Hebrew High School. The Bureau also provides a media center and teacher accreditation services. Representatives from the affiliate schools and religious congregational schools serve as members of the Bureau's board of trustees.

The records include correspondence, minutes of committee meetings, reports, financial records, scrapbooks, newspaper clippings, and publications of the Bureau and its affiliated schools. The materials in this collection are a major source of information on the development and organization of Jewish education in the Greater Cleveland area.

Finding Aid: Register in preparation.

Note: The original minute books of the Bureau of Jewish Education are maintained by the Bureau. Microfilm copies of the minutes are held by the American Jewish Archives at Hebrew Union College, Cincinnati, Ohio.

61 YESHIVATH ADATH B'NAI ISRAEL. Records, 1917-1975. 15 containers, 2 volumes (11.4 linear feet). Donated by the Yeshivath Adath B'nai Israel, 1977. MS 3834.

An Orthodox Hebrew afternoon school, the Yeshivath Adath B'nai Israel (YABI) was incorporated in 1917 to provide a religious education for unaffiliated Orthodox families and congregations without their own religious schools. In its early years YABI was financed completely by tuition payments and private contributions. In 1946, YABI affiliated with the Bureau of Jewish Education and became a beneficiary agency of the Jewish Community Federation.

The records include committee minutes, reports, correspondence, lists of names, financial accounts, and publications relating to the administration of the Yeshivath Adath B'nai Israel and its educational policies, programs, and goals. Also included are administrative records and correspondence between YABI and community organizations including the Bureau of Jewish Education and the Jewish Community Federation. The bulk of the material consists of records from the late 1940s through the early 1960s.

Finding Aid: Unpublished 18-page register.

62 MONTEFIORE HOME. Records, 1885-1965. 25 containers (31.3 linear feet). Donated by the Montefiore Home, 1975 and 1976. MS 3835.

Founded in 1882 by the Order of Kesher Shel Barzel, a Jewish fraternal order, the Montefiore Home was originally known as the Sir Moses Montefiore Kesher Home for Aged and Infirm Israelites. The Home's first structure on Woodland Avenue accommodated approximately sixty-five residents who were sixty-five years of age or older. Nearly forty years later Montefiore Home built a new and larger facility at Mayfield and Lee roads in Cleveland Heights. Since its establishment, Montefiore has become nationally known as a long-term care facility offering medical and nursing care, psychiatric and social casework services, occupational and physical therapy, and a sheltered workshop.

The records include historical materials on the organization of the Home, administrative files, correspondence, minutes of meetings, committee reports, personnel records, financial materials, and statistical studies pertaining to the status of residents of Montefiore. The collection also includes topical files relating to various aspects of work with the aged and to affairs in the Cleveland Jewish community, publications, newspaper clippings, and scrapbooks.

Finding Aid: Register in process.

63 IGNATZ KOENIG (1866-1925). Papers, 1888-1911. 2 folders (0.1 linear feet). Donated by Mrs. Florence Stein, 1980. MS 3836.

Ignatz Koenig was born in Budapest, Hungary. After serving in the Austro-Hungarian army for twelve years he immigrated to the United States and settled in Cleveland in 1898. In 1900 he married Mollie Rice. Koenig was a garment cutter at the Landesman-Hirschheimer Company from shortly after his arrival in Cleveland until 1924. As a member of the garment cutters union, he was involved in the Cleveland garment strike of 1911. Initially joining in the strike, Koenig soon returned to work. In 1924, he left the clothing factory to work in a men's furnishing

Manuscripts: Major Collections

Manuscripts: Major Collections

store, Spanye, Reich & Company, in which a relative was a partner.

The papers consist of letters (primarily in German, but accompanied by typescript English translations), and two identification books from Koenig's service with the Austro-Hungarian army. With the exception of one letter written by Mollie Koenig, all of the letters are from Koenig to his family. Koenig's family moved to Indianapolis, Indiana, as a precautionary measure following his return to work during the strike. The correspondence relates largely to the events of the strike and to various family matters.

64 EMANUEL STERN (b. 1910). Papers, 1931-1979. 3 folders (0.2 linear feet). Donated by Emanuel Stern, 1980. MS 3837.

Emanuel Stern, who was born in Cleveland, graduated from Collinwood High School in 1928 and attended Cleveland College. In 1932 he helped organize a Cleveland branch of Aleph Zadik Aleph, a youth chapter of the B'nai B'rith organization. He subsequently assumed the presidency of the Cleveland Heights Lodge of B'nai B'rith.

The papers consist primarily of letters, clippings, and printed programs relating to the establishment and early history of the Cleveland chapter of Aleph Zadik Aleph.

65 JEWISH BAKERS UNION, LOCAL 56. Records, 1924-1950. 13 volumes. Donated by Edward Pershey, 1980. MS 3858.

Local 56 was established in 1902. For many years the union was headquartered in the lower Woodland Avenue Jewish community from which it drew much of its membership. During the period 1910-1916, the union changed its local number from 56 to 50, returning to and retaining the local number 56 after 1917.

The records of the Cleveland local consist of membership and dues books and a receipt book. The volumes provide the name and address of each member of the union as well as data concerning his standing in the union.

66 PRINTZ-BIEDERMAN COMPANY. Records, 1914-1957. 1 container (0.5 linear feet). Donated by Arthur Jaffe, 1979. MS 3870.

The Printz-Biederman Company was established in Cleveland in 1893 by Moritz Printz, his sons Michael and Alexander, and his son-in-law, Joseph Biederman. Throughout its history the company specialized in the manufacture of women's coats which were marketed under the trademark "Printzess." The company sold its products nationally and by 1934 expanded into a large manufacturing facility, "Printzess Square," on East 61st Street near Superior Avenue. Printz-Biederman ceased operations in 1979.

The records consist primarily of minutes, reports, agreements, correspondence, and publications of various employee representative bodies in the company, 1914-1920. These included a house of representatives, senate, and a welfare committee, which addressed employee grievances and coordinated employee activities such as picnics and excursions. A small but significant body of material, including correspondence, reports, and agreements, reflects efforts by the International Ladies Garment Workers Union to organize this paternalistic operation in the mid-1930s. Included in these files are letters, telegrams, and copies of writings by Abraham Katovsky and David Dubinsky. The collection also contains printed material relating to the various styles of garments this company manufactured over the years.

67 HIRAM HOUSE NEIGHBORHOOD SURVEYS. Research Notes, 1976-1977. 1 container (0.2 linear feet). Donated by John J. Grabowski, 1977. MS 3871.

Hiram House social settlement served a neighborhood of Cleveland which was predominantly Jewish during the period 1896-1916. These surveys consist of address-by-address listings of residents in an approximately twenty-five square block area surrounding the settlement for the years 1896, 1906, 1916, and 1929. The surveys were compiled from data contained in Cleveland city directories for these years.

In addition to residents' names, the surveys note occupation and assumed nationality. Research notes maintained with the surveys provide tabulations of ethnic background and basic occupational level.

Note: See also entry 1.

68 MT. SINAI HOSPITAL. Scrapbooks, 1903-1968. 1 roll of microfilm.

In 1903, Mt. Sinai Hospital, which was earlier known as the Jewish Women's Hospital, was located on East 37th Street in Cleveland. In 1916, the hospital, which soon thereafter provided service to the general public, moved to its present location on East 105th Street.

These scrapbooks contain newspaper clippings, photographs, and some letters relating to the hospital and its activities over the years.

Manuscripts: Major Collections

Manuscripts: Major Collections

Note: The original scrapbooks (six volumes) are maintained by Mt. Sinai Hospital. The Western Reserve Historical Society holds only the microfilm.

69 ALBERT A. WOLDMAN (1897-1971). Papers, circa 1930-1970. 18 containers (28.0 linear feet). Donated by Mrs. Albert Woldman, 1972 and 1975. Acc. Nos. 360 and 573.

The papers of Albert A. Woldman, judge of the Cuyahoga County juvenile court, consist primarily of files relating to Woldman's research on Abraham Lincoln, general history, civil rights, and the juvenile court. Also included in this collection are reports and speeches; materials relating to the judge's books, *Lawyer Lincoln* (1936) and *Lincoln and the Russians* (1952); and other publications accumulated by Judge Woldman.

Note: Arrangement and description of this collection are not completed.

70 HOWARD M. METZENBAUM. Papers, 1974. 69 containers (100 linear feet). Donated by Senator Howard M. Metzenbaum, 1974. Acc. No. 477.

This collection consists of the subject and activities files of Senator Howard M. Metzenbaum, who was appointed to fill the unexpired term of William Saxbe of Ohio in 1974. The files, which consist mainly of constituent correspondence, relate to a variety of topics of national and local concern, including Jews in Syria, Israel, the Middle East, the Palestine Liberation Organization, and Soviet Jewry.

Finding Aid: Unpublished 69-page inventory.

Restrictions: Permission of Senator Howard M. Metzenbaum required.

71 HADASSAH, WOMEN'S ZIONIST ORGANIZATION, CLEVELAND CHAPTER. Records, circa 1910-1972. 1 container (0.5 linear feet). Donated by the Cleveland Chapter of Hadassah, 1976. Acc. No. 781.

The records of the Cleveland Chapter of Hadassah, founded in 1913, include two scrapbooks of correspondence, newspaper clippings, programs, brochures, and photographs and other miscellaneous materials. This organization provides medical assistance, primarily to Hadassah Hospital in Israel and, earlier, Palestine.

Note: Accessioning not completed; more material expected.

72 BARNETT R. BRICKNER (1892-1958). Papers, circa 1920-1958 (approximately 103 linear feet). Donated by Mrs. Barnett Brickner, 1977 and 1980. Acc. Nos. 1026 and 1426.

The papers of Barnett R. Brickner, Reform rabbi of Anshe Chesed Congregation from 1925 to 1958, and a prominent spokesman for the Cleveland Jewish community, include correspondence, sermons, radio scripts, articles, newspaper clippings, and general secretarial office files relating primarily to Rabbi Brickner's work at Euclid Avenue Temple and to his community and civic activities.

Note: The arrangement and description of this collection are not completed.

73 ANSHE CHESED CONGREGATION. Records, circa 1846-1970 (approximately 20.0 linear feet). Donated by the Fairmount Temple, 1980. Acc. No. 1425, et al.

Over the years, this congregation, chartered in 1842, was known as the Eagle Street Synagogue (1845), the Scovill Avenue Temple (1887), the Euclid Avenue Temple (1912), and, currently, the Fairmount Temple (1957). Originally Orthodox, Anshe Chesed had evolved into a Reform congregation by the mid-1870s.

The records include correspondence, financial and membership records, publications, and service bulletins. Also included are copies of sermons delivered by this congregation's rabbis: Michael Machol (1846-1914), who served from 1876 to 1906; Louis Wolsey (1877-1959), 1907 to 1924; and Barnett R. Brickner (1892-1958), 1925 to 1958.

Note: The arrangement and description of this collection are not completed.

74 LEON WIESENFELD. Papers, 1919-1967. 3 containers (1.5 linear feet). Donated by Mrs. Leon Wiesenfeld, 1977 and 1981. Acc. Nos. 941 and 81-36.

The papers of journalist Leon Wiesenfeld include correspondence in English and Yiddish, telegrams, certificates, programs, newspaper clippings, and a scrapbook. Included is a file of the *Jewish Voice Pictorial* from the years 1941 to 1967 which was published by Wiesenfeld and copies of two fictional works, *Broken Souls* (1919) and "Two Brothers" (1929). Approximately one-third of this collection consists of correspondence in Yiddish, Polish, and Russian addressed to Mrs. Sandra Lowy in care of Esther Wiesenfeld from relatives in Poland and Russia. The material dates from the late 1930s, early 1940s, and post-World

War II era, with some of the letters bearing Nazi censorial stampings.

Note: Arrangement and description of this collection are not completed.

75 JEWISH LIBRARY ASSOCIATION OF CLEVELAND. Records, 1955-1979. 1 container (0.5 linear feet). Donated by Miriam Leikind, 1981. Acc. 81-78.

Minutes, correspondence, membership lists and flyers relating to the activities of the Association, which is composed of librarians employed in synagogues, schools, and other agencies in the Greater Cleveland Jewish community.

Note: Arrangement and description of this collection are not completed.

76 BETH ISRAEL CONGREGATION. Records, 1915-1978. 4 containers (3.0 linear feet). Donated by Beth Israel (West Temple), 1981. Acc. 81-89.

Minutes, scrapbooks, publications, financial files, and photographs of this Reform congregation. Beth Israel (West Temple) is the only synagogue located on the west side of Greater Cleveland. Though most of the files date after 1950, the collection contains some earlier items which relate to B'nai Israel Congregation and the West Side Jewish Center, which preceded Beth Israel in serving the city's west side Jewish population.

Note: Arrangement and description of this collection are not completed.

77 HEIGHTS JEWISH CENTER. Records, 1925-1957. 1 container (0.5 linear feet). Donated by Mrs. Vera Kinsler, 1981. Acc. 81-129.

Primarily legal documents relating to property transfers and other real estate matters involving the Heights Jewish Center, an Orthodox congregation now located in University Heights, Ohio. The files were originally maintained by the congregation's counsel, Charles C. Goldman.

Note: Arrangement and description of this collection are not completed.

78 RABBI RUDOLPH M. ROSENTHAL (1906-1979). Papers, circa 1930-1979. 2 containers (1.5 linear feet). Donated by Mrs. Rudolph Rosenthal, 1980. Acc. No. 81-133.

The papers of Rudolph M. Rosenthal, rabbi of the Temple on the Heights (B'nai Jeshurun Congregation) from 1933 to 1976, include correspondence, speeches and sermons delivered by

Rosenthal and the notes he used in their preparation, certificates, temple bulletins, newspaper clippings, photographs, and other miscellaneous materials relating to his Conservative congregation.

Note: Accessioning not completed; more material expected.

79 HENRY L. ZUCKER (b. 1910). Papers, circa 1940-1977. 1 container (0.5 linear feet). Donated by Henry Zucker, 1979. Acc. No. 81-134.

Manuscripts: Major Collections

The papers of Henry L. Zucker consist primarily of correspondence, reports, minutes, and biographical materials produced during his service with the Jewish Community Federation of Cleveland. During the years 1946-1975, Zucker served as associate director, executive director, and executive vice president of this agency. Some materials relate to his service in other agencies such as the International Conference of Jewish Communal Service, the Welfare Federation of Cleveland, and the Joint Distribution Committee.

Note: Accessioning not completed; more material expected.

II. Manuscripts: Vertical File Collections

Each entry consists of the title under which the collection is catalogued, birth and death dates (for individuals), span dates for material in the collection, and a brief description of the contents.

Manuscripts: Vertical File Collections

80 DAVID PERETZ ADELMAN (d. 1925). Papers, 1910-1925. 1 folder (27 items). Includes copies of letters written by Adelman, while living in a Lithuanian shtetl, to his son Moishe-Josef in Cleveland.

81 MOSES ALSBACHER (b. 1805). Manuscript, 1839. 1 folder (1 item). Ethical testament presented to a company of Jews emigrating from Unsleben, Bavaria, to Cleveland. The testament, written by Lazarus Kohn, contains the names of the emigrants and of the Jews remaining in Unsleben as well as a reminder to the emigrants to preserve their Jewish faith.

82 MOSES ALSBACHER (b. 1805). Journal, 1864-1869. 1 folder. Journal of Moses Alsbacher containing penmanship exercises and birth and death dates of members of his family in Cleveland.

83 ESTEE ANEISZ FAMILY. Papers, 1886-1906. 1 folder (16 items). Includes letters, written primarily in Yiddish, by Estee Aneisz in Hungary to relatives and friends in the United States and Canada concerning family matters.

84 AVUKAH, ZIONIST YOUTH ORGANIZATION, ADELBERT AND WESTERN RESERVE CHAPTER, CLEVELAND, OHIO. Volume, 1930. 1 folder. Treasury book containing receipts, bills and financial notes, and drafts of several letters.

85 MOSES BASKIND. Article, 1972. 1 folder. A history of the Baskind family entitled "Thoughts on reaching the age of 77," with a foreword by Moses Baskind.

86 MARTIN BENJAMIN. Papers, 1967-1972. 1 folder (40 items). Includes brief writings on the Talmud by Benjamin's father, Isaac Benjamin.

87 ALFRED A. BENESCH (1879-1973). Papers, 1935-1955. 1 folder (5 items). Includes speeches and articles written by Benesch, attorney and member of the Cleveland board of education, concerning education and educational institutions.

88 HARRY BERNSTEIN (1856-1920). Papers, 1876-1920. 1 folder (7 items). Includes copies of the certificate of naturalization of Harry Bernstein, a Cleveland politician, and obituaries.

89 B'NAI B'RITH, LODGE NO. 1407, KINSMAN-SHAKER. Letters, 1944-1945. 1 folder (32 items). Letters written by servicemen during World War II.

90 LOEB COLMAN FAMILY. Papers, 1840-1914. 1 folder (13 items). Miscellaneous documents, including an indenture, power of attorney, bank book, and receipts.

91 CHARLES C. COLMAN FAMILY. Papers, 1869-1944. 1 folder (10 items). Includes receipts, railroad ticket stubs, and several autographs.

92 DAUGHTERS OF YAVNE, Cleveland, Ohio. Records, 1953-1969. 1 folder. Minutebook of this Orthodox Jewish organization that provided relief and baby clothes to the poor. In Yiddish.

93 FRIEDA BLONDIS DEMICK. Papers, 1956. 2 folders (6 items). Includes an article written by Demick, "My Journey to America," describing her emigration from Russia in 1914, and copies of newspaper articles pertaining to her reminiscences.

94 EUCLID JEWISH CENTER (Temple Ner Tamid). Records, 1929-1978. 1 folder (8 items). Includes letters and reports on the Jewish population of Euclid, Ohio, and the founding of this Reform congregation.

95 Z. GUKEREI FAMILY. Papers, 1939-1941. 1 folder (19 items). Primarily letters from family members in Lithuania to relatives in Cleveland during the period of Nazi conquest and occupation.

96 KAUFMAN HAYS (1835-1916). Papers, 1910. 1 folder. Includes a copy of an autobiographical account of this prominent Cleveland businessman and community leader.

97 HEIGHTS JEWISH CENTER. Records, 1969. 1 folder (4 items). Includes two copies of "The History of Heights Jewish Center" and copies of related articles about this Orthodox synagogue.

98 LIZA JAFFE. Letter, 1925. 1 item. Copy of the original and a typed translation of a letter written by Jaffe while living in the Soviet Union to her mother, Genessel Jaffe, residing in the United States.

Manuscripts: Vertical File Collections

Manuscripts: Vertical File Collections

99 MORITZ JOSEPH. Papers, 1899. 1 folder (2 items). Copy of a letter from Moritz Joseph to Mrs. Meyer Wiener regarding the donation of a house and lot to the Council of Jewish Women in Cleveland and a copy of a testimonial from the council to Moritz and Jetta Joseph on their golden wedding anniversary.

100 IGNATZ KLEIN FAMILY. Papers, 1895, 1971. 1 folder (2 items). Military service record of Ignatz Klein, a Hungarian immigrant, and a copy of the certificate of election of his son, William, former mayor of Bratenahl, Ohio.

101 ILONA AND MIHALY KLEIN FAMILY. Papers, 1944. 1 folder (3 items). Includes notes to Irene Klein from her parents Ilona and Mihaly written before they were taken by the Nazis from the Jewish ghetto of Ojpest, Hungary, and transported to Auschwitz.

102 LASZLO KRAUSZ. Article, 1965. 1 folder. A copy of an account by Laszlo Krausz of the visit of the Cleveland Orchestra to the Soviet Union in 1965.

103 LABOR ZIONIST ORGANIZATION, CLEVELAND, OHIO. Records, 1933-1934, 1948. 1 folder. Minutes, 1933-1934, of Zeire Zion and minutes, February-May, 1948, of Poale Zion Zeire Zion, branches of the Labor Zionist Organization.

104 LOUIS LAUFMAN FAMILY. Papers, 1881-1972. 1 folder (7 items). Miscellaneous documents, including a wedding certificate, power of attorney, and identity card.

105 HEIMAN LEDERMAN FAMILY. Papers, 1906-1913. 1 folder (5 items). Includes a notebook in Yiddish, a passport case, and inspection cards.

106 LLEWELLA SICKLES KEIM. Volume, 1901. 1 folder. Ledger book containing lists of wedding invitations.

107 ISAAC MILTREIGER FAMILY. Papers, 1923-1924. 1 folder (10 items). Includes affidavits in support of applications for visas.

108 OER CHODESH ANSHE SFARD. Records, 1904, 1944. 1 folder (2 items). Constitution and letter relating to this Cleveland Orthodox congregation.

109 TOBEY PENN. Article, n.d. 1 folder. A copy of "Raisin in My Soup," which details the life of a young Jewish girl growing up in the Woodland Avenue district of Cleveland in the 1920s.

110 ALLAN PESKIN. Article, 1965. 1 folder. A manuscript copy of "This Tempting Freedom," a monograph which describes the early years of Cleveland Judaism and the Anshe Chesed Congregation.

111 FELIX ROSENBERG FAMILY. Papers, 1840-1912. 1 folder (19 items). Includes copies of an application for naturalization, military service records, newspaper clippings, and various certificates.

112 NATHAN ROTHENBERG FAMILY. Papers, 1893-1927. 1 folder (8 items). Miscellaneous documents including a certificate of school attendance, diploma, passport, and certificates (in Russian).

113 SAM SAVINSKY FAMILY. Papers, 1924-1935. 1 folder (10 items). Includes passports, legal documents, and correspondence in Yiddish.

114 DANIEL J. SILVER. Sermons, 1967-1968. 2 folders (2 items). Copies of sermons entitled "Taking Stock of 1967" and "The Jewish Year in Review" delivered by Rabbi Daniel J. Silver.

115 ISIDORE STEINBERG. Articles, 1965. 1 folder (3 items). Reminiscences, including "YABI Recollections," concerning the history of Yeshivath Adath B'nai Israel, an Orthodox Hebrew school located in Cleveland.

116 OSCAR SOLOMON STRAUS (1850-1926). Letter, n.d. 1 item. A letter from Oscar Straus, chairman of the National Relief Committee based in New York City, to Edward M. Baker of Cleveland, concerning relief for the Jews in Russia.

117 SIMSON THORMAN. Certificate, 1866. 1 item. The certificate of naturalization issued by Frederick J. Prentiss, clerk of the court of common pleas of Cuyahoga County to Simson Thorman, former resident of Bavaria and the first Jewish settler in Cleveland.

*Manuscripts:
Vertical File
Collections*

Manuscripts: Vertical File Collections

118 GEORGE WASSER. Certificate, 1914. 1 folder. The declaration of intention of George Wasser, former resident of Russia, to become a United States citizen.

Appendix A: Photographs
1. Picture Groups

Picture groups include larger bodies of photographs maintained as units within the general picture collection. Arrangement is alphabetical by title of picture group.

Each entry consists of the title of the group, the number of containers, the reference access number, and a brief description of the contents.

Appendix A:
Photographs
Picture Groups

A1 JULIUS AMBER. 1 container. Picture Group 213. Portraits, views and postcards, circa 1930-1975, pertaining to the life of Julius Amber and to his work with the Jewish National Fund of Cleveland. Included are several photographs of awards dinners and banquets honoring Senator Hubert Humphrey, Senator Howard Metzenbaum, Congressman Charles Vanik, Congressman Louis Stokes, Congressman James Stanton, and television news commentator Dorothy Fuldheim.

A2 BELLEFAIRE. 7 containers, 2 oversize containers, 2 portfolios. Picture Group 154. Portraits of individuals and groups, views, miscellaneous photographs and albums, circa 1870-1970, of staff, students, and facilities of Bellefaire and the Jewish Orphan Asylum; and numerous photographs of activities that took place at these institutions.

A3 HARRY BERNSTEIN. 1 container. Picture Group 195. Portraits, views, and an album, circa 1905-1908, of Harry Bernstein, prominent Republican ward leader, his family and his associates. Included are two photographs of Bernstein at the Peoples Theater in the lower Woodland Avenue neighborhood of Cleveland as well as several general views of life along that thoroughfare in the early 1900s.

A4 SIGMUND BRAVERMAN. 2 containers, 1 portfolio. Picture Group 210. Portraits of Braverman and views and slides, circa 1950-1960, of his work as an architect. Included are views of Jewish religious buildings he designed in Cleveland, Akron, and Canton, Ohio, as well as structures in Alabama, Georgia, Iowa, Kentucky, Maryland, Massachusetts, Michigan, Nebraska, North Carolina, North Dakota, Pennsylvania, and Tennessee.

A5 CLEVELAND SECTION, NATIONAL COUNCIL OF JEWISH WOMEN. 1 container. Picture Group 118. Portraits, photographs, slides, and an album, circa 1920-1960, of the members and activities of the Cleveland Section. Included are pictures of Martha House, a home for young women established by the Council, the Council Thrift Shop, and entertainment events, such as the Council "Follies."

A6 MAX P. GOODMAN. 2 containers. Picture Group 171. Portraits and albums of photographs, circa 1890, pertaining to the activities, family and friends of Goodman, attorney and Cleveland city councilman.

A7 MOSES J. GRIES FAMILY. 1 container. Picture Group 192. Portraits, tintypes, and an album, circa 1880-1955, relating to Rabbi Moses J. Gries, members and friends of his family, and the related Hays and Beaumont families.

A8 HIRAM HOUSE, 7 containers. Picture Group 48. Portraits and views, 1896-1960, of the Hiram House social settlement, its camp, staff, and activities. Includes pictures of events which took place at the settlement during the early 1900s, when the area it served was the major Jewish neighborhood in Cleveland.

A9 JEWISH COMMUNITY CENTER. 3 containers. Picture Group 149. Portraits and views, circa 1910-1960, of the staff, members, activities, and facilities of the Jewish Community Center and its predecessor agencies, particularly the Council Educational Alliance and Camp Wise.

A10 JEWISH COMMUNITY EXHIBIT PHOTOGRAPHS. 12 oversize containers. Picture Group 186. Portraits, views, and miscellaneous photographs, circa 1860-1960, of Jewish neighborhoods, businesses, institutions, and community activities. All of the photographs in this picture group are mounted display copies of originals owned by the Western Reserve Historical Society or maintained in private collections. Many of the photographs in this picture group are reproduced in *Merging Traditions* (see entry B66).

A11 JEWISH DAY NURSERY. 1 container. Picture Group 209. Portraits and views, 1922-1972, of students, staff, and facilities of the Jewish Day Nursery of Cleveland, and several portraits of Miss Jeanette Sheifer.

A12 JEWISH WAR VETERANS, POST NO. 14. 1 container. Picture Group 189. Portraits and miscellaneous photographs, 1937-1973, pertaining to the members and activities of this veterans post headquartered in Cleveland, including views relating to the post's patriotic and service activities during World War II.

Appendix A: Photographs Picture Groups

Appendix A:
Photographs
Picture Groups

A13 JOSEPH AND FEISS COMPANY. 2 containers. Picture Group 175. Portraits and views, 1914-1950, of the facilities and employees of this clothing manufacturing firm, as well as views of employee recreation facilities and activities at the company during the 1920s and other aspects of the liberal administration of the company.

A14 MANUEL LEVINE. 1 container. Picture Group 204. Portraits and lithograph, 1912-1940, of Judge Manuel Levine, his family, and associates.

A15 DR. ALEXANDER MILLER. 1 container. Picture Group 198. Portraits, views, and surgical photographs and slides, circa 1950-1965, relating to Dr. Miller's military career and to his medical work in Vietnam and on the hospital ship *Hope*.

A16 ABRAHAM LINCOLN NEBEL. 1 container. Picture Group 163. Portraits, circa 1860-1965, of Abraham Lincoln Nebel, his family and friends and of members of prominent Jewish families from the Cleveland area, including the Peixotto, Richman, Cohen, Marx, and Davies families, and photographs of sites related to the history of these families.

A17 OAKWOOD CLUB. 2 containers, 1 portfolio. Picture Group 144. Portraits, other photographs, and albums, circa 1920-1969, of some of the members and activities of the Oakwood and Excelsior clubs. The albums, in particular, contain studio portraits of prominent Jews from the Cleveland community, including Morris Rohrheimer, Charles Eisenman, Charles Ettinger, Paul Feiss, Maurice Maschke, and Joseph R. Printz.

A18 SHERWIN BAKING COMPANY. 1 container. Picture Group 196. Portraits and views, circa 1930-1960, of members of the Sherwin family and exterior and interior views of the Sherwin Baking Company, including pictures of patriotic window displays arranged by the company during World War II.

A19 SAMUEL H. SILBERT. 2 containers, 1 portfolio. Picture Group 172. Portraits, circa 1920-1965, of Judge Samuel H. Silbert, his family and friends, and views of the homes in which the Silberts resided.

A20 STANDIFORD PHOTOGRAPH COLLECTION. 11 oversize containers. Picture Group 47. Mounted studio portraits, circa 1920-1940, of prominent Clevelanders including Alfred A. Benesch, Rabbi Barnett R. Brickner, Ezra Brudno, David H. Dietz, Paul Feiss, Salmon P. Halle, Manuel Levine, James Metzenbaum, and Rabbi Abba Hillel Silver.

A21 SELMA H. WEISS. 1 container. Picture Group 140. Portraits, views, and postcards, 1936, taken and collected by Selma Weiss during a trip to Europe and the Soviet Union; and an album of photographs, 1945, of Wakeman General Hospital, a Red Cross facility of which Miss Weiss was field director.

A22 ZIONIST ORGANIZATION OF AMERICA. 1 container. Picture Group 188. Portraits and miscellaneous photographs, 1966-1974, relating to the members and activities of the Cleveland branch of the Zionist Organization of America. A number of the portraits are of individuals honored by the ZOA, including Gerald R. Ford, Rabbi Abba Hillel Silver, and Congressman Charles Vanik; and of musical artists such as Itzhak Perlman and Jan Peerce.

Appendix A: Photographs
2. Portraits

Listings are alphabetical by name of subject.
Each photograph description is followed by an item count in parentheses and a file locator symbol:
- S Standard File
- T Tintype Collection
- C Cased Image Collection

Appendix A: Photographs Portraits

A23 PORTRAITS

Alsbacher, Julia (1)	C
Apple, Max (72)	S
Benesch, Alfred A. (14)	S
Benjamin, Leon (1)	S
Berman, Morris L., Family (15)	S
Brickner, Rebecca (Mrs. Barnett R.) (2)	S
Cohen, Max, Family (2)	S
De Harrack, Charles (7)	S
Demick, Frieda Blondis (1)	S
Feiss, Benjamin, and Richmond Families (25)	S
Feiss, Paul (1)	S
Feiss, Edith L. (Mrs. Paul) (1)	S
Friedman, Samuel (1)	S
Garber, Suggs (31)	S
Goldberg, Arthur J. (1)	S
Gries, Rabbi Moses J. (3)	S
Gries, Frances Hays (Mrs. Moses J.) (1)	S
Gries, Robert D. (2)	S
Gross, Louis N. (1)	S
Grossman, Mary BX. (32)	S
Hays, Kaufman (2)	S
Jaffe, Lester A. (1)	S
Klein, Eugene M., Family (7)	S
Klein, Ignatz, Family (7)	S
Klein, Ilona and Mihaly (1)	S
Koblentz, Max (1)	S
Laufman Family (3)	S
Levine, Manuel (16)	S
Lipson, Simon L., Family (1)	S
Metzenbaum, Howard (13)	S
Miller, Alexander (2)	S
Ratner, Albert, and Leonard Ratner (1)	S
Rivchun Family (12)	S
Rosenwasser, Marcus (2)	S
Sandin, Max (23)	S
Savinsky Family (3)	S
Shapiro, Ezra (2)	S
Shapiro, Sylvia (Mrs. Ezra)	S
Silver, Rabbi Abba Hillel (5)	S
Silverstein, Abe (1)	S
Silbert, Samuel (3)	S
Spira, Henry (1)	S
Ullman, Clara (1)	T
Ullman, Howard P. (2)	S
Ullman, Ludwig (1)	S

Ullman, Monroe A. (4)   S, T
Ullman, Morris (3)   S
Ullman, Rufus M. (3)   S
Ullman Family (10)   T
Weinberg, Joseph (17)   S

Appendix A:
Photographs
Portraits

Appendix A: Photographs
3. Views and Events

Listings are alphabetical by subject.
Each photograph description is followed by an item count in parentheses and a file locator symbol:
- S   Standard File
- O   Oversize File
- P   Postcard File

Appendix A:
Photographs
Views and Events

A24 Banquets
    Kinsman Jewish Center, 1950s (2)   O
    Jewish Welfare Fund Banquet, 1954 (8)   S
    Ninth Annual Banquet of the Rabbinical College
      of Telshe, 1950 (1)   O

A25 Buildings
    Jewish Community Federation of Cleveland, 1966 (2)   S

A26 Businesses
    Kletzkin Furriers, 1920s (2)   S
    Levy and Stearn, 1894 (1)   S
    Sherwin Baking Company, 1940s (1)   O
    Ullman, Einstein and Company, 1900 (1)   S

A27 Cemeteries
    Lansing Avenue Jewish Cemetery, 1971 (4)   S

A28 Clubs, Associations and Fraternal Organizations
    B'nai B'rith Youth Organization, 1950s (6)   S
    Cleveland Section National Council
      of Jewish Women, 1920s (5)   S, O
    Excelsior Club, 1910s (2)   P
    Hadassah, School of Instruction, 1951 (1)   S
    Jewish Boys Club, 1920s (2)   S
    Lincoln Literary Society, 1900s-1960s (15)   S, O
    Oakwood Club, 1920s (2)   S
    World Zionist Organization, 1920s (1)   S
    Young Hebrew Club, 1910s (1)   S

A29 Conventions
    Delegates at the First Zionist Convention in
      Cleveland, 1903 (1)   O
    First Annual Convention of the Ohio State
      Zionist Region, 1932 (1)   O

A30 Industries
    Cleveland Worsted Mills, 1910s, 1920s (2)   S, O
    L. N. Gross Company, 1930s (8)   O
    Lattin, Bloomfield & Co., 1910s, 1930 (17)   S
    Richman Brothers, 1910s (2)   S

A31 Music and Musicians
    Cleveland Jewish Band, 1915 (1)   S
    Cleveland Jewish Singing Society, 1930s (5)   S

First Jewish Russian Synagogue (Ohavei Emuna
   Congregation) Choir on Hill Street, 1898 (1)   S
Shaaray Torah Synagogue Choir, 1910s (1)   S

A32 Orphanages
Jewish Orphan Asylum, 1888-1910 (50)   S, O, P

A33 Schools
Central High School, 1890s-1920s (84)   S, O, P

A34 Social Service Agencies
Camp Wise, 1900s-1930s (4)   S
Council Educational Alliance, 1910s-1940s (4)   O
Hiram House, 1930s, (4)   S, O
Jewish Day Nursery, 1920s (4)   O
Jewish Family Service Association, 1940s-1960s (31)   S
Menorah Park, Jewish Home for Aged,
   1930s-1940s (18)   S, O

A35 Temples and Synagogues
Eagle Street Synagogue (Anshe Chesed
   Congregation), 1870s (1)   S
East 55th Street and Scovill Avenue Temple
   (B'nai Jeshurun Congregation), 1910s (1)   P
Euclid Avenue Temple (Anshe Chesed
   Congregation), 1910s-1940s (12)   S, O, P
Green Road Synagogue, 1970s (4)   S
Huron Street Synagogue (Tifereth Israel
   Congregation), 1880s (1)   S
Scovill Avenue Temple (Anshe Chesed
   Congregation), 1880s (2)   S
Shomrei Hadath Congregation, 1960s (1)   S
Suburban Temple, 1966 (1)   O
Tetiever Achim Anshe Sfard Synagogue, 1940s (8)   S
The Temple (Tifereth Israel Congregaton),
   1940s, 1960s (10)   S, P
Willson Avenue Temple (Tifereth Israel
   Congregation), 1890s, 1910s (11)   S, P

Appendix A:
Photographs
Views and Events

Appendix B:
Printed Materials
1. Organizational

Consists of pamphlet publications and annual reports issued by Jewish organizations in the Greater Cleveland area. Listing is alphabetical by name of organization.

Appendix B:
Printed Materials
Organizational

B1 AMERICAN HEBREW BENEVOLENT SOCIETY, CLEVELAND
Constitution and by-laws, 1965.

B2 CLEVELAND HEIGHTS HIGH SCHOOL, CLEVELAND HEIGHTS
Journal of Testimony; a living tribute to the victims of the Holocaust, 1975.

B3 CLEVELAND INSTITUTE OF JEWISH STUDIES, CLEVELAND
Brochure, 1959-1960.

B4 CLEVELAND JEWISH ORPHAN ASYLUM (BELLEFAIRE), CLEVELAND
Histories, 1868, 1893, 1903
Anniversary pamphlet, 1918
Miscellaneous items, 1906-1907

B5 CLEVELAND JEWISH SINGING SOCIETY, CLEVELAND
Histories, 1959, and undated
Miscellaneous items, 1915, 1925, 1927

B6 CLEVELAND JEWISH TERCENTENARY COMMITTEE, CLEVELAND
Cleveland and the Tercentenary, circa 1954

B7 EUCLID AVENUE TEMPLE (ANSHE CHESED CONGREGATION), CLEVELAND
Anniversary pamphlets, 1936, 1946
Yearbook, 1919-1920
Bulletin, 1954-1955
Miscellaneous items, 1919-1920, 1949

B8 EUCLID AVENUE TEMPLE ALUMNI ASSOCIATION, CLEVELAND
Bugle Call Rag (mimeographed publication), November 1942-March 1946

B9 EUCLID JEWISH CENTER (TEMPLE NER TAMID), EUCLID
History, 1951
Bulletins, 1958, 1960
Miscellaneous items, 1955 and undated

B10 FAIRMOUNT TEMPLE (ANSHE CHESED CONGREGATION), BEACHWOOD
    History, 1974
    Miscellaneous items, 1962, 1973

B11 FEDERATION OF THE JEWISH CHARITIES OF CLEVELAND
    (see also Jewish Community Federation of Cleveland)
    Annual reports, 1904-1910, 1912-1914, 1921

Appendix B:
Printed Materials
Organizational

B12 HEBREW FREE LOAN ASSOCIATION, CLEVELAND
    Constitution and by-laws, 1911

B13 HEBREW RELIEF ASSOCIATION, CLEVELAND
    (see also Jewish Family Service Association)
    Annual reports, 1898, 1910

B14 HEBREW SINGING AND BENEVOLENT ASSOCIATION, CLEVELAND
    Program, 1899

B15 HUNGARIAN BENEVOLENT AND SOCIAL UNION, CLEVELAND
    Anniversary pamphlet, 1891

B16 JEWISH COMMUNITY FEDERATION OF CLEVELAND
    History, 1975
    Yearbooks, 1951-1966
    Report of the Jewish Education Study Committee, 1976

B17 JEWISH FAMILY SERVICE ASSOCIATION, CLEVELAND HEIGHTS
    Annual report, 1978

B18 JEWISH ORTHODOX HOME FOR AGED, CLEVELAND
    Anniversary pamphlet, 1956

B19 JEWISH WAR VETERANS OF THE UNITED STATES, CLEVELAND POST 14
    Anniversary pamphlet, 1969

Appendix B:
Printed Materials
Organizational

B20 JEWISH WELFARE FEDERATION, CLEVELAND
(see also Jewish Community Federation of Cleveland)
Yearbooks, 1942, 1946-1950

B21 LEAGUE FOR HUMAN RIGHTS, CLEVELAND
Brochure, 1945

B22 LITTLE BUSY BEES SOCIETY, CLEVELAND
Program, 1893

B23 MIZRACHI WOMEN'S ORGANIZATION OF AMERICA, CLEVELAND
History, 1970

B24 MONTEFIORE HOME, CLEVELAND AND CLEVELAND HEIGHTS
Annual reports, 1882-1907
Bulletins, 1973-1975

B25 MT. SINAI HOSPITAL, CLEVELAND
Annual reports, 1977-1978

B26 PARK SYNAGOGUE (ANSHE EMETH CONGREGATION), CLEVELAND HEIGHTS
Bulletins, 1958, 1962
Miscellaneous items, undated

B27 SCOVILL AVENUE TEMPLE (ANSHE CHESED CONGREGATION), CLEVELAND
Anniversary pamphlet, 1896
Bulletin, 1908

B28 SHOMRE SHABOTH CONGREGATION, CLEVELAND
Constitution, undated

B29 TAYLOR ROAD SYNAGOGUE, CLEVELAND HEIGHTS
Anniversary pamphlet, 1954

B30 TEMPLE ON THE HEIGHTS (B'NAI JESHURUN CONGREGATION), CLEVELAND HEIGHTS
Constitution, 1957
Anniversary pamphlet, undated

B31 WARRENSVILLE CENTER SYNAGOGUE, SOUTH EUCLID
Anniversary pamphlet, 1971

Appendix B:
Printed Materials
Organizational

Appendix B: Printed Materials
2. Published and Unpublished Studies

Consists generally of biographical, autobiographical, and historical works germane to the Greater Cleveland Jewish community. Arrangement is alphabetical by author, editor, or title.

Appendix B:
Printed Materials
Published and
Unpublished Studies

B32 ANTINE, HENRY A. "Camp Alliwise; An Adventure in Democracy." Master's thesis, School of Applied Social Sciences, Western Reserve University, 1941.

B33 BRANDEIS, LOUIS DEMBITZ. *The Jewish Problem, How to Solve It: With a Biographical Sketch of Justice Louis D. Brandeis by Joseph Saslaw*. Cleveland: J. Saslaw, 1934.

B34 BROWN, ALBERT M. *My First Fifty Years in Social Work*. Cleveland Heights: By the author, 1974(?).

B35 CLEVELAND JEWISH CENTENNIAL COMMITTEE. *The Jewish Community in Cleveland: Historical Digest, 1837-1936*. Cleveland: By the Committee, 1937.

B36 *The Cleveland Jewish Society Book*, Vols. 1-6. Cleveland: The Jewish Independent Publishing Co., 1915-1922.

B37 COGSWELL, DEWITT R. (compiler). "The Ancestry of Robert Hays Gries and Lucille Dauby Gries." Typescript. Cleveland, 1965.

B38 GARTNER, LLOYD P. *History of the Jews of Cleveland*. Cleveland: Western Reserve Historical Society and the Jewish Theological Seminary of America, 1978.

B39 GAYNON, DAVID. "From the Shtetl to Cleveland: Cultural Continuity among Eastern European Immigrants, 1882 to World War I." Seminar paper, Case Western Reserve University, 1974.

B40 GRABOWSKI, JOHN J. "A Social Settlement in a Neighborhood in Transition: Hiram House, Cleveland, Ohio 1896-1926." Ph.D. dissertation, Case Western Reserve University, 1977.

B41 GREEN, HOWARD WHIPPLE. *Jewish Families in Greater Cleveland*. Cleveland: Cleveland Health Council, 1939.

B42 GREENSTEIN, SIMA. "Jewish National Religious Poems." Mimeographed. Shaker Heights, Ohio, 1958?

B43 GRIES, MOSES J. *The President's Address to the Central Conference of American Rabbis at the Twenty-Sixth*

Annual Convention, Charlevoix, Michigan, June 29, 1915. [1915].

B44 JEWISH THEOLOGICAL SEMINARY OF AMERICA, AMERICAN JEWISH HISTORY CENTER. *Proceedings of the Conference on the Writing of Regional History, With Special Emphasis on Religious and Ethnic Groups: Convened by Western Reserve University, Western Reserve Historical Society, and the American Jewish History Center of the Jewish Theological Seminary of America, Cleveland, December 1, 1955.* New York: By the Seminary, 1956.

B45 JOSEPH, FRANK E. (compiler). "Jewish Families, Cleveland." Mimeographed. Cleveland [1956].

B46 KLAUSNER, HELEN-ROSE (compiler). "Belonging to the Family Bruml." Mimeographed. Cleveland(?): n.d.

B47 LIPMAN, EUGENE J., and ALBERT VORSPAN (editors). *A Tale of Ten Cities: the Triple Ghetto in American Religious Life.* New York: Union of American Hebrew Congregations, 1962. Includes a chapter on the Jewish community of Cleveland by Sidney Z. Vincent.

B48 MELAMED, FRANCES. *Janova.* Cincinnati: Janova Press, Inc., 1976. Story of Jewish immigrant experiences based in part on stories from the author's family, some of whom resided in Cleveland.

B49 MORGENSTERN, JOSEPH. *I Have Considered My Days.* New York: YKUF Publishers, 1964. Part of this autobiography relates to the years the author spent in Cleveland.

B50 NATIONAL CONFERENCE OF JEWISH SOCIAL WELFARE. "Community Study of Cleveland." Mimeographed. Cleveland: 1944. Prepared for the joint annual meeting of the National Conference of Jewish Social Welfare, National Association of Jewish Center Workers, and the National Council for Jewish Education at Cleveland, Ohio, May 17-21, 1944.

B51 NEBEL, ABRAHAM (compiler). "Civil War Soldiers Buried in Cleveland Cemeteries, Also Jewish Civil War

Appendix B: Printed Materials Published and Unpublished Studies

Soldiers Who Enlisted in Cleveland and Outside of Cleveland." Electrostatic copy. Cleveland, n.d.

B52 PESKIN, ALLAN. *This Tempting Freedom: The Early Years of Cleveland Judaism and Anshe Chesed Congregation.* Cleveland: 1973.

B53 RUBINSTEIN, JUDAH. "The Jewish Press in Cleveland." Electrostatic copy. Cleveland, Ohio, 1974.

B54 RUBINSTEIN, JUDAH. "Jewish Suburban Population Movement in Cleveland and Its Impact on Communal Institutions." Mimeographed. Cleveland: Jewish Community Federation, 1957.

B55 SHARLITT, MICHAEL. *As I Remember: The Home in My Heart.* Shaker Heights, Ohio: Privately published, 1959.

B56 SILBERT, SAMUEL H. *Judge Sam.* Manhasset, N.Y.: Channel Press, 1963.

B57 SILVER, DR. ABBA HILLEL, MOSHE SHERTOK AND DAVID BEN-GURION. *The Jewish Agency before the United Nations.* New York: American Zionist Emergency Council, 1948?

B58 SILVER, ABBA HILLEL. [Holdings include nineteen published sermons and addresses relating to various Jewish and international topics, circa 1920-1948. Most of these publications were issued by The Temple (Tifereth Israel Congregation), Cleveland, Ohio.]

B59 SILVER, SAMUEL M. *Portrait of a Rabbi: An Affectionate Memoir on the Life of Barnett R. Brickner.* Cleveland: Barnett R. Brickner Memorial Foundation, 1959.

B60 SINGER, SIDNEY C. (compiler). "The Rosenwasser Family Tree." Electrostatic copy. Cleveland(?): n.d.

B61 SINGER, SIDNEY C. (compiler). "Two Hundred Years of Family History: The Story of Josef Kohn and His Descendants, 1744-1945." Electrostatic copy. Cleveland, n.d.

B62 SKOLNIK, LOUIS. *Selected Writings and Prose.* Holon, Israel: 1972. Written in Yiddish.

B63 SPERO, SHIMON ELIEZER. *Divrei Harav: Writings and Teaching of Rabbi Shimon Eliezer Spero.* Cleveland: The Young Israel of Cleveland, 1976.

B64 TABAKIN, HENRY. *Only Two Remained.* Cleveland: Robert Silverman, Inc., 1973.

B65 "Translation of the Alsbacher Document: Including List of Jews in Unsleben, Lower Franconia, Bavaria." Typescript. Cleveland, 1953(?).

B66 VINCENT, SIDNEY Z., and JUDAH RUBINSTEIN. *Merging Traditions: Jewish Life in Cleveland.* Cleveland: The Western Reserve Historical Society and the Jewish Community Federation of Cleveland, 1978.

B67 WIESENFELD, LEON. *Jewish Life in Cleveland in the 1920s and 1930s: The Memoirs of a Jewish Journalist.* Cleveland: The Jewish Voice Pictorial, 1965.

B68 WITTKE, CARL FREDERICK. *Reminiscence and Rededication.* Cleveland: Jewish Community Federation, 1954. Text of an address delivered before the fifty-first annual meeting of the Jewish Community Federation of Cleveland, December 5, 1954.

*Appendix B:
Printed Materials
Published and
Unpublished Studies*

Appendix B: Printed Materials
3. Newspapers and Periodicals

Consists of titles published in the Greater Cleveland area, including original and microfilm copies.

Frequency notations used in this section are as follow:
- d Daily
- w Weekly
- m Monthly
- q Quarterly

Appendix B:
Printed Materials
Newspapers
and Periodicals

B69 *Cleveland Jewish News.* w. October 30, 1964-October 5, 1979 (microfilm positive); October 5, 1979 to the present (original copy).

B70 *Friday, The Magazine of Jewish Life.* w., later m. March 16, 1934-November 1934.

B71 *Hebrew Observer.* w. July 5, 1889-July 4, 1890; September 2, 1897-November 24, 1898 (microfilm master negative and positive).

B72 *Jewish Guardian.* w. January 12, 1923-May 25, 1923. Partially in Yiddish.

B73 *The Jewish Independent.* w. March 9, 1906-October 23, 1964.

B74 *Jewish Review.* w. November 8, 1895-November 17, 1899 (microfilm master negative and positive).

B75 *Jewish Review and Observer.* w. November 24, 1899-December 26, 1958 (microfilm master negative and positive); January 2, 1959-August 28, 1964 (original copy).

B76 *Vare Shtime* (True Voice). w. March 20, 1914-February 26, 1915 (microfilm positive).

B77 *The Witness.* q. June 1911, December 1911, April 1912.

B78 *Yiddishe Tegliche Presse* (Jewish Daily Press). d. July 30, 1908-June 27, 1913 (microfilm positive).

B79 *Yiddishe Velt* (Jewish World). w. July 18, 1913-February 22, 1952 (microfilm positive).

Index

The numbers after index entries refer to the item numbers, not the page numbers. The letters A and B preceding a number identify the appropriate appendix. Letters and numbers in italics identify main entries.

Subject headings follow.

Aged
Anti-Semitism
Architects and Architecture
Authors
Bankers
Boycott, Anti-Nazi
Businessmen
Charities
Child Welfare
Civil Rights
Civil War
Clothing Industry
Community Centers
Discrimination
Economic Conditions
Education
Fascism
Fraternal Organizations
Genealogical Data
Health Agencies
Immigration and Immigrants
Industrial Relations
Journalism and Journalists
Judaism
Judaism, Conservative
Judaism, Orthodox
Judaism, Reform
Judges and Judiciary
Juvenile Delinquency
Labor and Laboring Classes

Law and Lawyers
Libraries
Literary Societies
Military
Music and Musicians
Nazism
Pacifism
Philanthropy, see Charities, Social Service
Physicians, see also Health Agencies
Poetry
Politics
Rabbis
Recreation
Religion
Social Life and Conditions
Social Service
Social Settlements
Social Workers
Socialism
Soviet Jewry
Travel
Women's Organizations
World War I
World War II
Yiddish Literature
Yiddish Newspapers
Yiddish Theater
Youth and Youth Movements
Zionism

75

Index

A

Adelman, David Peretz, *80*
Adelman, Moishe-Josef, 80
Aged, 3, 33, 62
Agnon Day School, 60
Agudas Achim Congregation, 37
Agudas B'nai Israel Congregation, 37
Akiva Hebrew High School, 60
Akron, A4
Alabama, A4
Aleph Zadik Aleph, Cleveland Branch, 64
Alsbacher document, *B65*
Alsbacher, Julia, A23
Alsbacher, Moses, *81, 82*
Amber, Julius, *58*, A1
American Association for Jewish Education, 44, 52, 60
American Bar Association, 13
American Civil Liberties Union, 2
American Hebrew Benevolent Society, *B1*
American Institute of Architects, Award of Merit, 50
Americanization, 1
American Jewish Congress, Cleveland Chapter, 52
American Jewish League for Israel, 44
American Red Cross, 12
American Zion Commonwealth, Inc., 52
Aneisz, Estee, Family, *83*
Anshe Chesed Congregation, 73, 110, B52. *See also* Fairmount Temple
Anshe Emeth Congregation. *See* Cleveland Jewish Center
Anshei Marmaresher Congregation. *See* Green Road Synagogue
Antine, Henry A., *B32*
Anti-Semitism, 4
Apple, Max, *45*, A23
Arab-Israeli crises, 32
Architects and architecture, 49, 50, 57, A4, A35
Architects Society of Ohio, Gold Medal, 50
Auerbach, Celia, 56
Auerbach, Charles, 56
Auschwitz, 101
Austro-Hungarian Army, 63
Austro-Hungarian Ladies' Aid Society, 27
Austria-Hungary, 49
Authors, 23, 69, 74
Avukah, Zionist Youth Organization, Adelbert and Western Reserve Chapter, Cleveland, Ohio, *84*

B

Baker, Edward M., 116
Baldwin Wallace College, 13
Bamberger Family, 21
Bank of Henry Spira. *See* Spira Savings and Loan Association
Bankers, 36
Baskind, Moses, 85
Bavaria, 81, 117, B65.
Beachwood, Ohio, 33, 34.
Beaumont Family, A7
Bellefaire, *16*, A2
Benesch, Alfred, A., *42,* 87, A20, A23
Ben-Gurion, David, *B57*
Benjamin, Isaac, 86
Benjamin, Leon, A23
Benjamin, Martin, 86
Berman, Morris L., *54*
Berman, Morris L., Family, A23
Bernstein, Harry, *88,* A3
Beth Hamedrosh Anshe Galicia. *See* Sinai Synagogue
Beth-Israel Congregation, 76
Biederman, Joseph, 66
Bikur Cholim Ladies Sick Aid Society, *20*
Black, Maurice, 5
Blacks, 1, 11
B'nai B'rith, 42, 64
B'nai B'rith, Cleveland Chapter, 21
B'nai B'rith, Grand Lodge District Two, 16
B'nai B'rith, Greater Ohio Council (Region), 59
B'nai B'rith, Heights Lodge, 59, 64
B'nai B'rith, Lodge No. 1408, Kinsman-Shaker, 89
B'nai B'rith, Southern Ohio Council, 59
B'nai B'rith Youth Organization, A28. *See also* Ohio B'nai B'rith Youth Organization
B'nai Israel Congregation, 76
B'nai Jeshurun Congregation. *See* Temple on the Heights
Bohemia, 42, 51
Boycott (Anti-Nazi), 4
Brandeis, Louis Dembitz, *B33*
Bratenahl, Ohio, 100
Braverman, Sigmund, *49,* A4
Brickner, Rabbi Barnett R., 72, 73, A20
Brickner, Rebecca (Mrs. Barnett R.), A23
Brith Emeth Congregation, 28
Broken Souls, 74

Brown, Albert M., *B34*
Brudno, Ezra, A20
Bruml Family, B46
Buber, Martin, 56
Budwig, Edward, Family, *41*
Bureau of Jewish Education, 28, 44, 45, 52, *60*, 61
Businessmen, 6, 8, 18, 28, 35, 41, 43, 45, 54, 96, A10, A18, A26
    See also Clothing industry

C

California, 41
Camp Alliwise, B32
Camp Henry Baker, 17
Camp Wise, 17, A9, A34
Canada, 53, 83
Canton, Ohio, 59, A4
Carnegie Institute of Technology, 49
Central High School, A33
Charities, 5, 7, 16, 20, 30, 31, 39, 92, 116
Chattanooga, Tennessee, 6
Chibas Jerusalem Congregation, 37
Child Welfare, 1, 12, 16, 17, 53, A2, A11, A32, B32
Children's Aid Society of Philadelphia, 12
Civil rights, 4
Civil War, 6, B51
Cleveland, A4
Cleveland Association for Nursery Education, 53
Cleveland Board of Education, 42, 87
Cleveland Board of Health, 51
Cleveland Chamber of Commerce, Committee on Benevolent
    Associations, 7, 39
Cleveland City Council, 42
Cleveland College, 64
Cleveland College of Jewish Studies, 60
Cleveland Community Chest, 39. *See also* United Torch Services
    of Greater Cleveland
Cleveland General Hospital. *See* St. Luke's Hospital
Cleveland Hebrew Schools, 8, 43, 44, 52, 60
Cleveland Heights, Ohio, 17, 38, 62, 97
Cleveland Heights High School, *B2*
Cleveland Immigration League, 48
Cleveland Institute of Jewish Studies, *B3*
Cleveland Jewish Band, A31
Cleveland Jewish Centennial Committee, *B35*
Cleveland Jewish Center (Anshe Emeth Congregation), 8, 43
Cleveland Jewish News, B69

Cleveland Jewish Singing Society, 8, A31, *B5*
The Cleveland Jewish Society Book, B36
Cleveland Jewish Tercentenary Committee, *B6*
Cleveland Law School, 13, 52
Cleveland Orchestra, 102
Cleveland Welfare Federation, 7
Cleveland Worsted Mills, A30
Clothing industry, 22, 55, 66, A13, A30
Cohen Family, A16
Cohen, Max, Family, A23
Cogswell, DeWitt R., *B37*
Colman, Charles C., Family, *91*
Colman, Loeb, Family, *90*
Commercial Law League of America, 13
Commonwealth Oil Company, 18
Community centers, 3, 17, A9
Community Fund. *See* United Torch Services of Greater Cleveland
Confederate States of America, Army, 6
Council Educational Alliance, 3, 15, 17, 29, A9, A34
Council Gardens, 3
Council of Jewish Women, 99
Cuyahoga County Bar Association, 21
Council Thrift Shop, A5

D

Daughters of Yavne, *92*
Davies Family, A16
De Harrack, Charles, A23
Demick, Frieda Blondis, *93*, A23
Dietz, David H., A20
Discrimination, 4
Dubinsky, David, 66

E

Eagle Street Synagogue, 73, A35
Eagle Wholesale Grocery Company, 8
East 55th Street and Scovill Avenue Temple, A35
Economic conditions, 5, 9, 15, 22, 30, 67
Ecuador, 40
Eddy Road Jewish Center, 24
Education, 3, 16, 29 , 42, 56, 60, 61, 87, 115, A33
Einstein, Leopold, 6
Einstein, Siegfried, *19*
Eisenman, Charles, A17

Index

Index

Elyria, Ohio, 59
England, 57
Erster Galizianer Unterstützungs Verein, 9
Ettinger, Charles, 5, A17
Euclid, Ohio, 94
Euclid Avenue Temple (Anshe Chesed Congregation), 21, 72, 73, A35, *B7*
Euclid Avenue Temple Alumni Association, *B8*
Euclid Jewish Center (Temple Ner Tamid), 94, *B9*
Eugene M. Klein and Associates, 28
Europe, 35, 51, 54, A21
Excelsior Club, 14, A17, A28

F

Fairmount Temple (Anshe Chesed Congregation), 28, 54, 72, 73, *B10*
Farband Labor Zionist Organization, Branch 45, 57
Fascism, 4
Federation for Charity and Philanthropy, 7
Federation for Community Planning, 7, 39
Federation of Jewish Charities, 7, 39
Federation of the Jewish Charities of Cleveland, *B11*
Feiss, Benjamin, and Richmond Families, A23
Feiss, Edith L. (Mrs. Paul), A23
Feiss, Julius, 22
Feiss, Paul, 22, A17, A20, A23
Feiss, Richard, 22
Fellowship of Reconciliation, 2
First Jewish Russian Synagogue (Ohavei Emuna Congregation), A31
Ford, Gerald R., A22
Forest City Lodge (Masonic), 21
Fraternal organizations, 27, 89, A28
Friday, The Magazine of Jewish Life, *B70*
Friedman, Samuel, A23
Fuldheim, Dorothy, A1

G

Gan Yavne, 44
Garber, Simon, Haiman, Gutfield, Wertheimer, and Friedman, 52
Garber, Suggs, 52, A23
Gartner, Lloyd P., *B38*
Gaynon, David, *B39*
Genealogical data, 18, 82, 85, B37, B45, B46, B60

Georgia, A4
German-American Bund, 4
Germany, 4, 6, 19. *See also* Bavaria
Glenville neighborhood, 8, 43
Gmilus Chassodim Society, 5
Goldberg, Arthur J., A23
Goldman, Charles C., 77
Goldman, Harry, 16
Goldsmith, Jacob, 22
Goldsmith, Joseph, Feiss and Company, 22
Goodman, Max P., 56, *A6*
Goodman, Max P., Family, *21*
Grabowski, John J., *B40*
Green, Howard Whipple, *B41*
Green Road Synagogue, 38, A35
Greenstein, Sima, *B42*
Greensboro, North Craolina, 6
Gries, Frances Hays (Mrs. Moses J.), 35, A23
Gries, Lucille Dauby, B37
Gries, Moses, J., Family, 35, A7
Gries, Rabbi Moses J., 35, A23, *B43*.
Gries, Robert D., A23
Gries, Robert H., 35, B37
Gross and Dallet. *See* L. N. Gross Company
Gross, Louis N., 55, A23
Grossman, Mary B., *13*, A23
Gukerei, Z., Family, 95

H

Hadassah, 56; School of Instruction, A28
Hadassah, Women's Zionist Organization,
 Cleveland Chapter, *71*
Halle, Salmon P., A20
Harvard University, 42, 50, 56
Hays Family, A7
Hays, Frances. *See* Gries, Frances Hays
Hays, Kaufman, 35, *96*, A23
Health agencies, 62, 68
Hebrew Academy, 60
Hebrew Free Loan Association, 5, *B12*
Hebrew Observer, *B71*
Hebrew Relief Association, 12, 30, 42, *B13*. *See also* Jewish
 Family Service Association
Hebrew Singing and Benevolent Association, Cleveland, *B14*
Heights Jewish Center, 38, 77, 97
Hill House, 3

Hiram House, *1*, 48, *A8*, A34, *B40*
Hiram House Neighborhood Surveys, 67
Hope, 40, A15
Humphrey, Hubert, A1
Hungarian Benevolent and Social Union, Cleveland, *B15*
Hungarian Jews, 10, 13
Hungarian Ladies' Aid Society, 27
Hungary, 27, 36, 38, 63, 83, 100, 101
Huron Street Synagogue, A35

I

Immigration and immigrants, 1, 2, 3, 4, 5, 17, 19, 27, 36, 48, 81, 93, 105, 111, 112, 113, 117, 118, B39, B65
Independent Oddfellows, 27
Indianapolis, Indiana, 63
Industrial relations, 22, 55, 63, 66, A13
International Conference of Jewish Communal Service, 79
International Ladies Garment Workers Union, 66
Iowa, A4
Israel, 32, 44, 45, 46, 56, 57, 70, 71
Italians, 1, 11

J

Jaffe, Genessel, 98
Jaffe, Lester A., A23
Jaffe, Liza, *98*
Jewish Bakers Union, Local 56, 65
Jewish Boys Club, A28
Jewish Children's Bureau, 39
Jewish Community Center, 3, *17*, 39, *A9*
Jewish Community Council, 44, 56
Jewish Community Council, Cultural Department, 17
Jewish Community Exhibit Photographs, *A10*
Jewish Community Federation of Cleveland, 17, 42, 45, 52, 54, 60, 61, 79, A25, *B16*. *See also* Federation of Jewish Charities
Jewish Convalescent and Rehabilitation Center. *See* Jewish Convalescent Home
Jewish Convalescent Home, 20
Jewish Day Nursery, 53, *A11*, A34
Jewish Family Service Association, *30*, 39, 42, A34, *B17*
Jewish Guardian, B72
The Jewish Independent, B73
Jewish Library Association of Cleveland, 75
Jewish National Fund, 8, 52, 58, A1
Jewish National Fund of Cleveland, 52

Jewish Orphan Asylum (Home), 16, 42, 50, 51, A2, A32, B4
Jewish Orphan Asylum Magazine, 16
Jewish Orthodox Home for Aged, *B18. See also* Menorah Park
Jewish Orthodox Old Home. *See* Menorah Park
Jewish Review, B74
Jewish Review and Observer, B75
Jewish Social Service Bureau, 15, 30
Jewish Theological Seminary, 52
Jewish Theological Seminary of America, American Jewish History Center, *B44*
Jewish Vocational Service, *15*
Jewish Voice Pictorial, 74
Jewish War Veterans of the United States, 31
Jewish War Veterans, Post No. 14, *31, A12,* B19
Jewish Welfare Federation, *B20. See also* Jewish Community Federation of Cleveland
Jewish Welfare Fund Campaign, 28, A24
Jewish Women's Hospital. *See* Mt. Sinai Hospital
Jewish Young Adult Bureau, 17
John Huntington Polytechnic Institute, 50
John Marshall Law School, 56
Joint Distribution Committee, 28, 79
Joseph and Feiss Company, 22, *A13*
Joseph, Frank E., *B45*
Joseph, Jetta, 99
Joseph, Moritz, 22, 99
Journalism and journalists, 8, 74, B53, B67, B69-79
Judaism, 18, 56, 60, 81, 86, 110, B44, B52, B63, B65
Judaism, Conservative, 78
Judaism, Orthodox, 9, 10, 24, 25, 26, 33, 37, 38, 61, 73, 77, 92, 97, 108, 115
Judaism, Reform, 34, 35, 72, 73, 76, 94
Judge Sam, 23
Judges and judiciary, 13, 23, 48, 69, A14, A19, B56
Juvenile delinquency, 69

K
Katovsky, Abraham, 66
Keim, Llewella Sickles, *106*
Kent, Ohio, 55
Kentucky, A4
Keren Hayesod-United Israel Appeal, 44
Kesher Shel Barzel, Order of, 62
Kichler Company, 54
Kinsman Jewish Center, A24
Kinsman Road, 17

Index

Klausner, Helen-Rose, *B46*
Klein, Eugene M., Family, 28, A23
Klein, Ignatz, Family, *100,* A23
Klein, Ilona and Mihaly, Family, *101*
Klein, Ilona and Mihaly, A23
Klein, Irene, 101
Klein, William, 100
Kletzkin Furriers, A26
Knesseth Israel Congregation, 26, 37
Koblentz, Max, A23
Koch, Caufman, 22
Koch, Goldsmith and Company, 22
Koch, Goldsmith, Joseph and Company, 22
Koch, Levi, Mayer and Company, 22
Koenig, Ignatz, 63
Koenig, Mollie, 63
Kohn, Josef, B61
Kohn, Lazarus, 81
Krausz, Laszlo, *102*

L

Labor and laboring classes, 2, 22, 63, 65
Labor Zionist Organization, Cleveland, Ohio, *103*
Ladies Benevolent Society, 3
Landesman-Hirschheimer Company, 63
Lansing Avenue Jewish Cemetery, A27
Lattin, Bloomfield & Co., A30
Latvia, 23, 52
Laufman Family, A23
Laufman, Louis, Family, *104*
Law and Lawyers, 13, 21, 23, 42, 44, 48, 52, 56, 58, 87, A6
Lawyer Lincoln, 69
League for Human Rights, 4, *B21*
Lederman, Heiman, Family, *105*
Levi, Jacob, 22
Levine, Manuel, 48, *A14,* A20, A23
Levy and Stearn, A26
Libraries, 75
The Lincoln, 29
Lincoln, Abraham, 69
Lincoln and the Russians, 69
Lincoln Literary Society, 29, A28
Lipman, Eugene J., *B47*
Lipshitz, David, 8
Lipshitz, Rabbi Sander, 8

Lipson, Simon, 8
Lipson, Simon L., Family, 8, A23
Literary societies, 29
Lithuania, 80, 95
Little Busy Bees Society, Cleveland, *B22*
L. N. Gross Company, 55, A30
Loeb, Samuel, 22
Lorain, Ohio, 59
Lowy, Mrs. Sandra, 74

M

Machol, Rabbi Michael, 73
Marmaresher Jewish Center. *See* Green Road Synagogue
Martha House, A5
Marx Family, A16
Maryland, A4
Maschke, Maurice, A17
Massachusetts, A4
Mayer, Adolph, 22
M. D. Shanman Company, 43
Meadville, Pennsylvania, 22
Meistergram Company, 54
Melamed, Frances, *B48*
Menorah Park, Jewish Home for Aged, 33, A34
Merging Traditions, A10
Metzenbaum, Howard M., *70, A1,* A23
Metzenbaum, James, A20
Mexico, 41
Michigan, A4
Middle East, 70
Military, 2, 6, 31, 40, 54, 63, 100, 111, A12, A15
Miller, Alexander, *40, A15,* A23
Miller, Ellen, 40
Miller, Shin, *11*
Miltreiger, Isaac, Family, *107*
Mizrachi Women's Organization of America, Cleveland, *B23*
Montefiore Home, 62, *B24*
Morgenstern, Joseph, *B49*
Mount Pleasant neighborhood, 24
Mt. Sinai Hospital, 40, 51, 68, *B25*
Music and musicians, 102, A31

N

National Conference of Jewish Social Welfare, *B50*
National Council of Jewish Women, 3

Index

Index

National Council of Jewish Women, Cleveland Section, 3, 17, A5, A28
National Relief Committee, 116
Nazism, 4, 31, 74, 95, 101
Nebel, Abraham Lincoln, *18*, A16, B51
Nebel, Emmanuel, 18
Nebel Manufacturing Company, 18
Nebraska, A4
Neshkin, Samuel, *47*
Newark, New Jersey, 23, 57
New York City, 116
New York School of Social Work, 12
North Carolina, A4
North Dakota, A4
Northeastern Ohio Council, 59

O

Oakwood Club, *14, A17*, A28
Oer Chodesh Anshe Sfard Congregation, *108*
Ohavei Emuna Congregation. *See* First Jewish Russian Synagogue
Oheb Zedek Congregation, 27, 37
Ohio Bar Association, 21
Ohio B'nai B'rith Youth Organization, 59
Ohio Northern University, 44
Ohio State Zionist Region, First Annual Convention, A29
Orthodox Old Home. *See* Menorah Park

P

Pacifism, 2
Palestine, 52, 71
Palestine Liberation Organization, 70
Park Synagogue (Anshe Emeth Congregation), 52, *B26*
Peerce, Jan, A22
Peixotto Family, A16
Penn, Tobey, *109*
Pennsylvania, A4
Peoples Theater, A3
Perlman, Itzhak, A22
Peskin, Allan, *110, B52*
Philadelphia, Pennsylvania, 6
Philanthropy. *See* Charities; Social service
Physicians, 40, 51, A15. *See also* Health agencies
Pinski, David, 57
Poetry, B42

Poland, 5, 9, 44, 58, 74
Politics, 21, 70, 88, A3, A6
Printz, Alexander, 66
Printz-Biederman Company, *66*
Printz, Joseph R., A17
Printz, Michael, 66
Printz, Moritz, 66

Q

Quality Thread Company, 54

R

Rabbinical College of Telshe, Ninth Annual Banquet, A24
Rabbis, 35, 72, 73, 78, 114, A7, B59, B63
Ratner, Albert, A23
Ratner, Leonard, A23
Recreation, 17
Religion, 81, B65
Rice, Mollie. *See* Koenig, Mollie
Richman Brothers, A30
Richman Family, A16
Rickman, Hannah, 27
Rickman, Samuel, 27
Rochester, New York, 53
Rivchun Family, A23
Rohrheimer, Morris, A17
Rosenberg, Felix, Family, *111*
Rosenthal, Rabbi Rudolph M., 78
Rosenwasser Family, B60
Rosenwasser, Marcus, *51*, A23
Rothenberg, Nathan, Family, *112*
Rubinstein, Judah, *B53*, *B54*, *B66*
Russia, 2, 5, 8, 25, 43, 47, 48, 54, 55, 57, 74 , 116, 118. *See also* Soviet Union

S

St. John's Hospital, 51
St. Luke's Hospital, 51
Saslaw, Joseph, B33
Savinsky Family, A23
Savinsky, Sam, Family, *113*
Saxbe, William, 70
Schaffner, Cecile, 28
Scovill Avenue Temple (Anshe Chesed Congregation), 73, A35, *B27*

Index

Index

Shaaray Torah Congregation, 37
Shaaray Torah Synagogue Choir, A31
Shanman, Esther, 43
Shanman, Morris, *43*
Shapiro, Ezra, *44*, A23
Shapiro, Sylvia (Mrs. Ezra), A23
Sharlitt, Michael, *B55*
Sheifer, Jeanette, *53*, A11
Sherith Israel of Mount Pleasant, *24*
Sherith Jacob Congregation, 24
Sherith Jacob Israel Congregation, 24
Shertok, Moshe, *B57*
Sherwin Baking Company, *A18*, A26
Sherwin Family, A18
Shomrei Hadath Congregation, *10*, A35
Shomre Shaboth Congregation, *B28*
Silber and Gross. *See* L. N. Gross Company
Silbert, Samuel, H., *23*, *A19*, A23, *B56*
Silver, Rabbi Abba Hillel, 4, A20, A23, *B57*, *B58*
Silver, Rabbi Daniel J., *114*
Silver, Samuel M., *B59*
Silvershirts, 4
Silverstein, Abe, A23
Sinai Synagogue, *9*
Singer, Sidney C., *B60*, *B61*
Sir Moses Montefiore Kesher Home. *See* Montefiore Home
Skolnik, Louis, *57*, *B62*
Skolnik, Max, 57
Social life and conditions, 2, 11, 14, 41, 63, 80, 83, 95, 98, 109, A3, A8, A10, A17, A24, A28, B36, B48, B49, B55, B64, B66, B67
Social service, 1, 3, 7, 15, 16, 17, 30, 33, 39, 46, 62, 71, 79, A2, A5, A8, A9, A34, B50. *See also* Charities
Social settlements, 1, 17, 67, A8, B40
Social workers, 1, 12, B34
Socialism, 57
Sons of Isaac Association, 27
Soviet Jewry, 31, 70
Soviet Union, 12, 34, 98, 102, A21. *See also* Russia
Spanye, Reich & Company, 63
Spero, Shimon Eliezer, *B63*
Spira, Henry, *36*, A23
Spira International Express Company, 36
Spira Savings and Loan and Associaton, 36
Standiford Photograph Collection, *A20*
Stanton, James, A1
Starr, Benjamin, 42

Steinberg, Isidore, *115*
Stern, Emanuel, 59, *64*
Steubenville, Ohio, 59
S. Thorman and Company, 41
Stokes, Louis, A1
Straus, Oscar Solomon, *116*
Suburban Community Hospital, 40
Suburban Temple, *34*, A35
Syria, 70

T

Tabakin, Henry, *B64*
Talmud, 56, 86
Taylor Road Synagogue, 26, *37*, *B29*
The Temple (Tifereth Israel Congregation), 34, 35, A35
Temple Ner Tamid. *See* Euclid Jewish Center
Temple on the Heights (B'nai Jeshurun Congregation), 78, *B30*
Tennessee, A4
Tetiever Achim Anshe Sfard Synagogue, A35
Tetiever Ahavath Achim Anshe Sfard Congregation, *25*
Tetiever Social Benefit Society, 25
This Is Cleveland, 4
Thorman, Esther, 41
Thorman, Simson, 41, *117*
Travel, 12, 35, 36, 51, A21

U

Ukraine, 56
Ullman and Company, 6
Ullman and Einstein Realty Company, 6
Ullman Brothers, 6
Ullman, Clara, A23
Ullman, Einstein and Company, 6, A26
Ullman, Emanuel, 6
Ullman Family, A23
Ullman, Howard P., A23
Ullman, Ludwig, A23
Ullman, Monroe A., 6, A23
Ullman, Morris, A23
Ullman, Morris, Family, *6*
Ullman, Rufus M., 6, A23
United Appeal. *See* United Torch Services of Greater Cleveland
United Jewish Appeal, 56
United Jewish Religious Schools, 28, 60
United States Army, 40, 54

Index

United States Senate, 70
United Torch Services of Greater Cleveland, 7
University Heights, Ohio, 16, 77

V

Van Heusen Corporation, 22
Vanik, Charles, A1, A22
Vare Shtime, B76
Vietnam, 40, A15
Vincent, Sidney Z., B47, *B66*
Vorspan, Albert, *B47*

W

Wagner Family, 21
Wakeman General Hospital, A21
War Resisters League, 2
Warrensville Center Synagogue, 24, 25, *B31*
Washington, D. C., 12
Wasser, George, 118
Weinberg, Joseph, *50*, A23
Weinberg, Teare and Herman, 50
Weiss, Selma H., *12*, *A21*
Welfare Association for Jewish Children, 12
Welfare Council of Cleveland, 39
Welfare Federation of Cleveland, 39, 79. *See also* Federation for Community Planning
West Side Jewish Center, 76
West Temple. *See* Beth Israel Congregation
Western Reserve University, 50, 56
Western Reserve University, School of Applied Social Sciences, 30
Wiener, Mrs. Meyer, 99
Wiesenfeld, Esther, 74
Wiesenfeld, Leon, *74*, *B67*
Willson Avenue Temple, A35
Wilson, Woodrow, 2
The Witness, B77
Wittke, Carl Frederick, *B68*
Woldman, Albert A., 69
Wolsey, Rabbi Louis, 73
Women's American Organization for Rehabilitation Through Training, Cleveland Region, *46*
Women's organizations, 3, 20, 46, 56, 71, 92, A5
Women's Zionist Organization, 53
Woodland Avenue, 11, 16, 17, 36, 62, 65, 109, A3

Workmen's Circle School, 60
World War I, 2, 54
World War II, 4, 12, 14, 74, 89, A12, A18
World Zionist Organization, A28

Y

Yeshivath Adath B'nai Israel, 60, *61*, 115
Yiddishe Tegliche Presse, B78
Yiddishe Velt, B79
Yiddish literature, B62
Yiddish newspapers, B72, B76, B78, B79
Yiddish theater, 47, A3
Young Hebrew Club, A28
Young Israel Congregation, 10
Young Men's Hebrew Association, 21
Youngstown, Ohio, 6
Youth and youth movements, 29, 59, 64, 84

Z

Zionism, 8, 32, 44, 45, 52, 56, 57, 58, 71, 84, 103, A1, A22, B57
Zionist District of Cleveland, 44
Zionist Organization of America, 8, 44
Zionist Organization of America, Cleveland Branch, A22
Zionist Organization of America, National Administrative Committee, 52
Zionist Organization of America, Temple District, 32
Zionist Organization of America, Temple on the Heights District, 32
Zionist Organization of America, District of Cleveland, 32
Zucker, Charles and Peter, 21
Zucker, Henry L., 79

OF THIS FIRST EDITION OF
A GUIDE TO JEWISH HISTORY SOURCES
IN THE
WESTERN RESERVE HISTORICAL SOCIETY
SEVEN HUNDRED AND FIFTY COPIES HAVE BEEN
PRINTED AND BOUND BY THE
LAKE SHORE PRESS OF CLEVELAND, OHIO
THE TEXT IS SET IN VARIOUS SIZES OF CALEDONIA
THE PAPER IS MOHAWK SUPERFINE
THE COVER IS BECKETT CAMBRIC BAMBOO